'rye, DVM, MS

Mutts

Everything about Selection, Care,
Nutrition, Breeding, and Diseases
With a Special Chapter on
Understanding Mixed-bred Dogs

With Drawings by Frank McLaughlin
and Photographs by Well-known Photographers

BARRON'S

Dedication:

To Brucye, Lorraine, Erik, Bice, and Noah, and to the many half-mutt, half-mongrel dogs with whom we have shared such warm and gratifying companionship.

All inquiries should be addressed to:
Barron's Educational Series, Inc.
250 Wireless Boulevard
Hauppauge, New York 11788

Library of Congress Catalog Card No. 88-34978

International Standard Book No. 0-8120-4126-7

Library of Congress Cataloging in Publication Data

Frye, Fredric L.
    Mutts : everything about selection, care, nutrition, breeding, and diseases with a special chapter on understanding mixed breed dogs.

    Includes Index.
    1. Dogs. 2. Dogs—Diseases. I. Title.
SF427.F79 1989   636.7   88-34978
ISBN 0-8120-4126-7

Printed and Bound in Hong Kong

456   4900   9876543

About the Author:

Dr. Fredric L. Frye is Clinical Professor of Medicine at the School of Veterinary Medicine of the University of California (Davis) and Attending Staff Clinician at the Davis Animal Hospital. A recipient of the Practitioner's Research Award of the American Veterinary Medical Association, he is the author of more than 200 papers and articles dealing with dogs, cats, reptiles, and invertebrates—among other subjects. His books include *Schnauzers* (Barron's); *First Aid For Your Dog* (Barron's); *First Aid For Your Cat* (Barron's); *Husbandry, Medicine and Surgery in Captive Reptiles*; *Biomedical and Surgical Aspects of Captive Reptile Husbandry*; and *Phyllis, Phallus, Genghis Cohen and Other Creatures I Have Known.*

Photo Credits:

D. J. Hammer: page 9 top right; page 27 top right, bottom; page 45; page 46 top left
Ray D. Kopen: page 28 bottom; page 46 bottom left; back cover to right
R. Lauwers: inside front cover; page 9 top left, bottom left and right; page 10; page 28 top right; page 46 top right, bottom right; page 64 bottom left and right; inside back cover
Aaron Norman: front cover
Wim van Vught: page 27 top left; page 28 top left; page 63; page 64 top left and right; back cover top left, bottom

Illustrations:

Michele Earle-Bridges: pages 18, 19, 20, 21, 23 34, 38
Karen English-Loeb: pages 42, 68, 70

Advice and Warning:

This book is concerned with selecting, keeping, and raising mixed breeds. The publisher and the author think it is important to point out that the advice and information for mixed-bred dog maintenance applies to healthy, normally developed animals. Anyone who acquires an adult dog or one from an animal shelter must consider that the animal may have behavioral problems and may, for example, bite without any visible provocation. Such anxiety-biters are dangerous for the owner as well as the general public.

Caution is further advised in the association of children with dogs, in meetings with other dogs, and in exercising the dog without a leash.

Contents

Foreword

When I was first approached about writing guidebooks on specific breeds of dogs, I agreed to write about only those breeds with which I have had experience as an owner. My first such book was *Schnauzers.* Shortly after it went to press, a plea was made to the editorial staff of Barron's Educational Series for a book on nonpurebred dogs. Clearly the "mutts," "mongrels," "smorgaspuppies," "57 varieties," and "all-Americans" (among other popular nicknames for nonpedigreed dogs) have their devoted followers. No specific dog breed has been, nor is presently, as popular as the mixed breed, or mutt.

We obtained our first mixed-bred dog when I was about ten years old. During the Great Depression, my family could barely afford to feed a dog (let alone purchase one with a pedigree). Nevertheless, they obtained a splendid pet for me at the local animal shelter. I have since shared my homes with a succession of both purebred and crossbred dogs of more than the proverbial 57 varieties! Some of these noble creatures were adopted as a consequence of my being a veterinarian. Occasionally, my clients would request euthanasia for their pets because their living arrangements no longer permitted a dog. Some patients that I had watched grow from puppyhood to young adulthood were available for adoption and, when no one else offered to take them in, my wife Brucye and I would find our family increased by one more furry newcomer.

Brucye and I had been married for barely two months when our first mixed breed took up residence with us. At the time I was enrolled in summer courses and we were living in a tiny apartment near the UCLA campus in Westwood Village. We (I) had already amassed a menagerie of one mynah bird, a South American "bird-eating" spider whose legs spanned about 10 inches, and an (*un*descented) spotted skunk. Our wee beasties only aggravated the overcrowded situation. In a moment of weakness (mine), we went to the pound and we (I) chose an adult and thoroughly immense ginger-colored male half-mastiff, half-golden retriever. It was obvious that this magnificent creature had inherited its head from its mastiff parent for its dimensions approached those of a nail keg. Expressive great brown eyes looked out on the world from beneath a mildy wrinkled black mask. Two huge pendant jowls descended and framed his squarish face. Perhaps this creature's most outstanding feature was his magnificent tail: whenever he was walking or running, this appendage was carried elevated at an angle of about 35 degrees above the horizontal. Long golden-red "feathers" spread out from a central axis of the tail in a flag-like fashion. While awake and lying down, he would wag this large tail, making resonant thumping sounds on the wooden floor.

Our two children grew up with several different dogs of uncertain lineage. Large ones, small ones, shaggy and smooth, long-haired and short-haired. Our household was seldom without its canine complement, nor assorted cats, a Toggenberg goat, a crippled screech owl named "Upjohn," several loquacious parrots, an orphaned shrike, and "exotic" animals such as slow lorises, bats, hedgehogs, an ocelot, snakes, lizards, tortoises, frogs, newts, scorpions, and spiders. Occasionally our various dogs came into contact with some of these animals and, after the initial novelty wore off, they invariably ignored their fellow household creatures (except the skunk).

Acknowledgments

The efforts of Barron's Educational Series to produce and distribute authoritative and well-illustrated reference and guidebooks for a reasonable price must, in my opinion, be acknowledged. In today's publication market it is not easy to find authors who have the expertise and experience—and the ability and time—to write substantive books in the field of animal science and husbandry. Having written several books that were published

Foreword

by other presses, I have a special appreciation for the support, craftsmanship, and sensitivity of Donald Reis, Sally Strauss, and the entire editorial staff of Barron's.

A special thank you to my wife, Brucye, whose editorial efforts were applied to the manuscript before submission to the copy editors. As I wrote the text, I was oft reminded of her forbearance for sharing our homes with so many different creatures.

Credit is due to Dr. Carol A. Himsel who read the manuscript and whose constructive suggestions were incorporated. Having served as a peer reviewer for several scientific journals, I understand how much time and effort can be expended to make someone else's work more valuable. I am most grateful for the illuminating perspective of a valued colleague.

Fredric L. Frye, DVM, MS

Understanding Your Mixed-bred Dog

History of the Dog

The dog family, or canidae, consists of the domestic dog, *Canis familiaris*; the wolf, *Canis lupus* (and others); the coyote, *Canis latrans*; the dingo, *Canis dingo*; the jackal, *Canis aureus*; the Cape or bush dog, *Lycaon pictus*; the fox, *Vulpes fulva, V. vulpes* (and others), as well as the fennec, the dog raccoon, the maned wolf, and the dhole.

In some cases, domestic dogs crossbred with other canids will yield fertile hybrid offspring. This is what happens when domestic dogs, wolves, coyotes, or dingos are mated with each other. Presently there are some breeding experiments attempting to crossbreed the cape dog and domesticated dogs. Domestic dogs and foxes do not produce hybrid puppies.

It is now known that primitive man domesticated canid carnivores slightly earlier than ruminants (sheep, goats, reindeer, wild oxen, and so on). These early canids served their human companions as guards against animal and human predators and regularly joined in the hunt. Paleontological and archeological studies have shown that prehistoric humans were accompanied on their hunting expeditions by the primitive animals that were destined to become "dogs" as we now know them. Cave art found in Europe and North Africa depicts hunters and rather contemporary dog-like canids. It is now generally accepted that the dog was domesticated at least 10,000 years ago, perhaps somewhat earlier. More than one authority has suggested that the domestication of man and the dog occurred simultaneously. This was a mutually beneficial process, in contradistinction to forceful captivity. In a symbiotic alliance, the dog aided in food gathering and protection and the humans provided shelter, sharing food and community.

These "protodogs" were most likely obtained as young puppies and, like their present day descendants, soon imprinted upon their human captors. Being natural communal pack animals, most canids will yield to a dominant individual. In the course of time, certain positive behavioral and physical traits were selected and, with purposeful inbreeding, definite breed characteristics were developed. Today, breeds as diverse as the Chihuahua and Great Dane can be mated (albeit with some intervention to help accommodate their physical size differences) and produce viable and fertile offspring that will bear the genetic contribution and physical endowments of both parents.

I have been fortunate in having had several opportunities to travel widely. During several of these trips I was able to observe semidomesticated "pariah" dogs in India, the Philippine Islands, Thailand, Burma, and Mexico. Additionally, I once treated a feral dog from Chile that was "rescued" from a refuse heap where it had been subsisting on rats. More recently, my wife Brucye and I had the opportunity to examine dogs belonging to native Americans living in Taos Pueblo, New Mexico. The ancient ancestors of these dogs are represented in the superb petroglyphs pecked into the surface of lava rocks near Albuquerque. The members of the Taos Pueblo community have been living there for well over 1,000 years, and actually may have been continually present for as long as 3,000 years. The truly fascinating thing about all of these dogs is that each has come to resemble a common creature characterized by a short yellow ochre to golden-brown coat, long legs, straight ear flaps that usually tip over at their ends, and a slightly upward curving tail. This pattern appears to have been so successful that it has been repeated through much of the temperate and tropic areas of human occupation. It seems that left to random breeding over a sufficient period of time, the domestic dog will revert to a common type.

Even the dogs that we now recognize as pure breeds were at one time crossbred and only became purebred by the intervention of man's selective breeding to concentrate, and thereby enhance, certain desired physical and/or behavioral characteristics. Currrently, there are very few dogs that resemble their primitive ancestors. Examples are the malamute and husky, the Australian dingo, the

South African cape, bush, or hunting dog, and the dhole, native to the Indian subcontinent.

Many of the physical, behavioral, and vocal characteristics of the malamutes and huskies closely resemble those of the North American and Siberian timber wolves. Perhaps it would be more accurate to describe these dogs as "races" instead of "breeds" and, indeed, some have been accorded the status of distinct species and subspecies although they can be crossbred with each other as well as with the domesticated dog and other members of the genus *Canis.*

The Nature of the Mixed Breed

Because the domestic dog has been developed by selective inbreeding for so long and for so many varied purposes, there is no single breed characteristic that is common to all mixed-bred dogs. Because of the immutable laws of genetic dominance and recessiveness, some physical, physiological, and behavioral traits will segregate into recognizable characteristics. Body size; leg length and degree of straightness; head shape; jaw length; haircoat color; length and degree of curliness and texture; ear flap shape, length and erectability; eye color and shape; sight acuity; stamina; scent detection ability; herding ability; retrieving ability; tail pointing; swimming ability; running speed; cart and sled drayage; voice (or lack of one); and personality traits are only some of the characteristics that humans have selected in the dogs that share their homes, hearths, farms, and workplaces. The Chinese crested, Mexican hairless, and Chihuahua were bred to be of convenient size in order to be consumed as food for their human companions; the former two have the extra "advantage" of being essentially naked. Today, these are valued as pets by people who would recoil in horror at the thought of eating members of their "family."

Today with well over one hundred recognized breeds from which to draw genes, it is impossible to predict what any litter of mixed-bred puppies might look or behave like when they mature. To make matters more complicated, a litter may have been sired by more than one male because dogs, being social creatures, may seize the opportunity to mate with almost any female in heat that will accept their ardent advances. The fact that a bitch already may have mated with a successful suitor does not isolate her from the attentions of other male dogs in her immediate neighborhood. Some litters of puppies may look like poodles; others may appear to be terriers; while others might remind the owner of that evening nine weeks previously when the neighbor's dachsund paid his nocturnal respects!

Generally outbred or crossbred dogs tend to be especially intelligent creatures. It is no accident that most circus and nightclub dog acts usually feature mongrel-type troupers.

Characteristic Behavior Patterns

Vocal Communications

Almost all dogs possess a voice. One exception is the Basenji: this compact and robust dog, which originated in Africa, does not bark *per se*, but squeals. The loudness of the bark or growl usually depends upon the size of the dog. Full volume sounds emitted by a large dog are replete with authority and command the immediate attention of household residents in case invited or uninvited persons arrive.

Small mixed breed dogs, like so many of the terrier-type breeds, tend to be more apt to bark, especially at the approach of strangers and other dogs. A small dog can, by its aggressiveness, command respect.

Depending upon the circumstances, other vocalizations can be joyful barking when a favored family member returns from an absence; yelps of pain; short barks and growls when feeling playful; howls at the sound of an emergency vehicle's siren; growls at intruders; and (particularly in puppies)

Understanding Your Mixed-bred Dog

miscellaneous whimpers and whines.

Small dogs usually confine their vocalizations to sharp barks. All dogs can, and should be trained not to bark incessantly.

Body Language

Stereotyped body language is an effective way for dogs to communicate effectively with people and each other. One of the most recognizable non-vocal communications is tail wagging. The manner in which the tail is carried also indicates the emotional state of dogs. A tail carried at a jaunty angle, or wagging slightly like a waving flag is a sure sign of canine contentment. A lowered tail that is tucked between the rear legs is a certain signal that the dog is either in the immediate presence of what it considers a dominant creature, or is cowering in wary expectation of punishment. Even dogs whose tails have been surgically docked can convey their emotions by the way they wag their abbreviated tail. By drawing back their lips as they wag their tails, some dogs actually smile; others smile with their tails alone!

Nonvocal messages of how a dog feels at any given moment are also displayed by the carriage of the ears. Surgically cropped ear flaps (pinnae),—rarely seen in mixed breeds—are much less mobile than natural, uncropped ear flaps. When content or while investigating something within their domain, dogs with upright pinnae tend to carry their ears erect or with only the outer third bent forward by their own weight. Dogs tend to allow their ears to droop against the tops and sides of the head when they are unhappy, fearful, or unwell. Heavy pendant ears, which under the best of circumstances never stand erect, are typical of mixed breeds descended from spaniels, retrievers, and hounds.

When the dog becomes agitated, the hairs (called "hackles"), if sufficiently long, become erect on the top of the neck and just in front of the root of the tail. This behavior may be a remnant of prehistoric times when confrontations were much more common. Each of the potential combatants appears larger, and thus more formidable by the heightened silhouette.

In an obvious display of bliss at being noticed, some dogs, particularly the smaller ones, often "dance" about on their feet.

Facial Expressions

The facial expression of a dog who is content reflects interest in its surroundings. At the first sign of anything novel, the ears are immediately elevated and the eyes scan intently for visual cues. The nasal openings flare in an attempt to detect unfamiliar scents.

Dogs stirred to aggression, may curl their lips, exposing the teeth, particularly the incisors and canines. The lips may be drawn even farther apart and the mouth held open, fully exposing the teeth and tongue, which is curled and held away from the incisors. The ears are carried in a flattened position. The dog may either withdraw or attack, given the opportunity. If the situation is not relieved and escape is impossible, the mouth is opened further, the growls become louder and more forceful, and the ears point forward toward the object of the aggression.

The foreheads and eyebrows of some terriers, schnauzers, sheep dogs, Irish wolfhounds, and others can add to nonvocal expression; just prior to attacking, the brows become furrowed which imparts a squint to the eyes.

Most dogs generally are not especially aggressive, and resort to this behavior only when severely provoked or are acting to protect their human family's territory and possessions.

Depending on their ancestry, mutts come in all shapes and sizes—from the smallest toy-size creatures to huge animals bred from Great Danes or St. Bernards. Mutts' coats are equally varied, ranging from short-haired and smooth to long and shaggy.

Understanding Your Mixed-bred Dog

Scent Marking

Dogs "stake-out" their territory by scent marking objects along their boundaries. This is accomplished in two ways: urine, which is deposited onto surfaces such as trees and shrubbery; and anal scent, which is deposited onto formed stools as they pass through the anus. The anal scent is secreted by paired, bean-shaped glandular sacs situated at openings into the anal canal at the four o'clock and eight o'clock positions.

This normal behavior of scent marking must be modified and redirected to a more suitable area outdoors than territory that is within your dwelling. By walking your dog on a leash, it can establish its own territory in the neighborhood. Your dog may have to share its new territory with other dogs, but that only reinforces each dog's zeal to mark objects and, thus, the bladder and anal sacs may be emptied more completely. As each vertical or horizontal "signpost" is encountered, the dog will sniff it to find out what messages have been left since his or her last visit. A tail wag signals a friendly "notice"; a growl indicates an unfriendly "letter."

Considerations of Social Dominance

A single dog in a household will usually consider itself submissive to its human owner. When more than one dog is in the family, it is normal for one of the dogs to assert its dominance over the other. A very submissive dog exhibits its deference by rolling over on its side or back and releases a variable amount of urine, signalling the dominant animal that it is primary. This indicates that an attack is unnecessary.

The colors of mixed-bred dogs reflect all of the colors found in the canine rainbow: black, white, brown, tan, red, etc.—as well as two-color and three-color mixtures.

Insecure dogs often roll over and urinate in the presence of their owners, particularly when any effort is made to pick up the dog or to discipline it. To an aggressor dog, the message is clear. To humans, the message is interpreted as only another mess to clean up. With confidence gained as a consequence of the owner's patience and consistent *correction* of misbehavior, most dogs will outgrow this trait swiftly.

The Sense Organs

Dogs appear to possess scent, hearing, and taste senses superior to their human friends. Dogs descended from hunting breeds such as the greyhound, whippet, saluki, and Afghan hound generally have excellent sight; their ancestors have been bred for centuries to chase very fast prey such as hares. Because taste is so closely related to smell it is not surprising that the sense of taste appears to be more acute in the canine than in humans. Only touch is more highly developed in humans than in dogs, but dogs do not need to rely on the this sense in their everyday dealing with their environment.

From Puppy to Adult Dog

The mixed-bred puppy changes quite a bit from the time of birth to weaning, which occurs at about five to six weeks. Even greater changes occur from weaning to young adulthood. The newborn multiplies its bulk four to fivefold during the first six weeks, as its muscles, skeleton, internal organs, and coat grow at a tremendous rate. During this critical growth period, the caloric intake in proportion to body weight exceeds that of the mature dog, which needs only to maintain its weight.

(The nutritional requirements for your mixed-bred puppy will be discussed in the chapter on Nutrition.)

A puppy should be obtained around the seventh

Understanding Your Mixed-bred Dog

The naturally warm relationship between a child and her cross-bred dog.

week of life, when socialization, or the adaptation of a puppy to human beings in the absence of the puppy's mother, begins. At this age it will transfer its allegiance to humans rather than to dominant dogs, as would be the case with a normally pack-socialized animal. Beyond the ten- to twelve-week age period, the human-dog social bonding is less readily achieved. For this reason, some young dogs raised from puppyhood to adulthood with little or no close contact with humans make unsatisfactory companion animals.

The age of puppies at sexual maturity is variable, just as it is in humans. Females reach early sexual maturity at five to seven months of age. Males generally attain sexual maturity several months later, and most are capable of siring puppies by the time they are ten to twelve months old. By the time of early puberty, male dogs (sometimes also females) will begin to lift one leg when they urinate. Interestingly, just as humans may be right- or left-handed, dogs tend to favor one leg over the other.

For most small mixed-bred dogs, middle age occurs at around eight to eleven years. The onset of middle age for larger mixed-bred dogs is usually a year or two earlier. Some slight dullness might be noted in their eyes. This mild cloudiness of the crystalline lenses of the eyes is a normal consequence of aging and usually does not lessen eyesight substantially. The lenses may become progressively opaque as the dog ages, but usually this is a very gradual process with which most dogs can readily cope. At about twelve years, as the dog reaches late middle age, its hearing may become less acute, just as its owner's hearing does at an equivalent biological age. This is a gradual result of aging and usually is of little consequence.

Aging dogs, like aging humans, may develop arthritis, heart disease, dental problems, diabetes, and tumors. Regular health-maintenance examinations by your trusted veterinarian will help insure a long and satisfactory life for your loved pet. Dogs of all breeds are now enjoying longer and healthier lives because of advances in veterinary medicine.

Contact with the World and Other Dogs

Bonding with your mixed-bred dog is vitally important. Also, it is essential that your dog *knows* that it is a dog, not a short four-legged human wearing a fur coat. As with purebred dogs, mixed-bred dogs should have contact with other dogs so they can learn to relate to nonhuman beings when encountered outside home territory.

After being properly immunized against infectious diseases, a young puppy should be taken outdoors to learn about the world. It is vitally important that the vaccination series has been completed before exposing a puppy to other dogs. These learning experiences will be more comfortable for all concerned if a leash and training collar that will not injure its tender neck is used. By becoming accustomed to wearing a collar and being led on a leash, the puppy will begin its early obedience training during its youth. Simple commands can be learned at this time. By the time the puppy is half grown, it should have mastered those manners that make any dog a positive part of your life.

Behavioral Disturbances

Some dogs develop psychological abnormalities, which may resemble similar disturbances in humans. Some breeds appear to carry a genetic predisposition for some of these behavioral traits. Because of their genetic diversity, most crossbred dogs seem free fortunately of these dominant heritable disturbances. Mixed-bred dogs may, like other specific dog breeds, exhibit special fondness for one member of the family over the rest, many animal observers note. It is almost unheard of, though, for the dog to display open aggression toward a household resident. Those very rare instances where this occurs can almost always be traced to mistreatment of the dog by that person. Most mixed-bred dogs are not inherently vicious, but their militant protective instincts can be released under some circumstances.

Obtaining a Mixed-bred Dog

Large or Small?

Many people consider mixed-bred dogs of any size or shape to be equal to, or superior to purebred dogs for canine companions. Often the size of housing determines which size of dog to adopt. If part of the decision rests upon the prospective dog's role as a watchdog, the larger mixed-bred dog usually has a bark with more authority. However, many smaller mixed-bred dogs possess a sharp bark and their ability to protect territory is often quite sufficient. This is especially true of dogs of part-terrier heritage.

The smaller mixed-bred dogs are easier to pick up, as necessary, whereas it requires more strength to lift a large dog. While being walked on a leash, the small dog that suddenly bolts at the sight of some distraction, like a running cat or squirrel, is unlikely to upset its owner. Of course, the smaller dog eats less, eliminates a smaller volume of urine and feçes, is much easier to bathe and groom, and requires much less space for its sleeping quarters. Automobile trips are far less crowded, and vacationing with a small dog is far less trying than with a large canine. Whereas some hotels and motels are unwilling to accept any dogs, others will allow their guests to register with small dogs. For those who spend much of their time aboard boats (most mixed-bred dogs of any size appear to enjoy water), or in recreational vehicles, the smaller size mixed-bred dogs are a sensible choice.

Although not invariably the case, small mixed-bred dogs tend to live longer lives than large mixed-bred dogs. And when everything is considered, the smaller dog will cost much less to maintain than larger dogs.

A Puppy or Mature Dog?

Watching a dog grow from puppyhood to adulthood under your guidance is one of the delights of pet ownersip. It will also require much effort and time on your part. The young puppy is a "clean slate": any habits that it develops will be acquired while it is in your care.

When it first enters your home, the older dog brings with it its own repertoire of learned behavior. This can save you a great deal of time and trouble. For example, an older dog will almost undoubtedly be fully housebroken. However, as time goes by other positive and negative habits are likely to emerge. Unfortunately, fixed behavioral disturbances are apt to remain lifelong, no matter how hard you work to correct them. The mature dog may not have been socialized properly during its critical seventh to tenth week teachable period. And, even if properly socialized, some mature dogs find it very difficult to adjust to new surroundings.

Male or Female?

Because the manner in which a dog is treated by you and others in your household will determine its response to humans, dogs of either sex can become affectionate and very suitable companions. In spite of widespread misconceptions, it cannot be demonstrated that males or females offer advantages over one another; nevertheless. Each sex has its own staunch advocates.

Generally, male dogs grow to a somewhat larger size than bitches. Adult male dogs are more persistent than females in scent marking their territories, although both will display this behavior to some extent. If a male mixed-bred dog detects the scent of a bitch in heat, he will react to that nearly irresistible stimulus by trying to reach the source of that scent cue; a simple screen door is no barrier when primal urges are inflamed. Although entirely normal, sexually aroused male dogs may display habits that are considered socially unacceptable in polite company. Unless you have some valid reason for not neutering your male, there are some compelling reasons to consider doing so just before he is one year old. This subject is discussed at length on page 50. With proper care, nutrition, and exercise, the neutered male dog lives a longer, more healthy life than he would if he had not been surgically altered and does not develop tumors or other diseases of the testicle or prostate gland, nor is he likely, later in life, to develop perineal hernias or perianal gland tumors.

At about the age of seven months, bitches usually come into their first estrus. This onset of sexual maturity may be slightly earlier or may be delayed by a month or two. Dogs usually keep themselves clean, but some discharge may stain carpeting or upholstery. Protective devices similar to infants' panties, which are fitted with a pocket into which a cotton gauze pad is inserted, can be used to prevent both soilage and accidental breeding by an attentive male. Chlorophyll-containing tablets available from veterinarians also will, if administered *before* a heat period, greatly diminish the sexually attractive female scent. These measures are not contraceptives and can be defeated by a particularly resourceful male dog. Oral contraceptive drugs are available from your veterinarian, but may cause unwanted side effects in some bitches.

Unless you wish to mate your bitch and raise her puppies, she should be spayed before her very first heat period. Myths about this subject hold that all bitch puppies should be allowed to either experience one or two estrous cycles or bear at least one litter of puppies before being spayed. Actual physiological studies and common sense agree that this is poor advice. As a veterinary surgeon, I can see no valid reason to allow a bitch to achieve full sexual maturity and then reverse the process and induce future potentially serious ovarian hormone-deficiency effects afterward. My own formal research in comparative cancer pathology and research of my colleagues here and abroad have shown conclusively that spaying a bitch before her very first estrus reduces the probability tremendously of breast cancer later in life. Even those few breast tumors that may develop in a small number of spayed bitches are usually benign and not life-threatening. Diseases of the ovaries and uterus and many disorders affecting the vagina are prevented

in females that have undergone the ovariohysterectomy (spay) operation.

Where to Obtain a Puppy

There are three primary sources of mixed-bred dogs: pet shops, private parties who just "happen to have some puppies," or animal shelters.

Reputable pet shops are an excellent source of mixed breeds *if* the dealer chooses to offer them. The problem is that most shops limit their offerings to purebred dogs. Exceptions are sometimes made for an unusually attractive litter, which would therefore be well worth your consideration. The most common environment is a large cardboard carton filled with appealing puppies and attended by a teary-eyed child whose feelings at having to part with the pups are very obviously more than slightly ambivalent.

Ideally, you would want to examine the home environment from which your prospective puppy comes. If you find it clean and the dogs well fed, you have the added assurance that the bitch's owners cared enough for their animals to provide them with a hygienic place in which to live.

Shelters offer puppies and mature dogs. Should you be captivated by one of the latter, read the suggestions on page 16 and the warning on the copyright before making a commitment.

You may find that your veterinarian knows of the availability of fine adult dogs or puppies. Also he or she may advise you *not* to select a dog or puppy from a particular source because it may be known to be infected with an infectious disease.

What Traits to Look for in Selecting a Puppy

Given the opportunity to choose from a wide variety of very similar animals, some people will

Obtaining a Mixed-bred Dog

pick the smallest, most feeble, wretched, or even deformed individual—the so-called "runt of the litter." Following are some suggestions on how to select a strong and sound puppy that will grow into an adult dog with whom you will be sharing many happy and healthful years.

One should specifically look for a lively, alert, even mildly aggressive puppy who is playing an active role in the litter. It should be responsive to gentle handling and possess a clean, moist nose pad, bright inquisitive eyes, and have reasonable coordination in its movements.

It is a myth that only healthy dogs have cold, wet nose pads. It is important that the nostrils be free of mucus, as should the eyelids. There must be no hint of coughing. The mouth and oral cavity should be examined to ensure that the hard palate is intact and that there are no gross dental abnormalities. The coat should be clean and free from any wastes. Although most young puppies have little pot bellies, they should not be excessively distended.

The new puppy should be full of life and express intense interest in its surroundings and in you as its potential new owner and companion.

The Age of the Puppy at the Time of Selection

By the time they reach six to six and a half weeks of age, puppies should be fully weaned. Before they are taken away from their dam, it is beneficial for them to nibble prepared puppy chow, cottage cheese, unflavored yogurt, and drink skim or cultured buttermilk. Other dairy items should not be fed because they may promote food allergies, and mineral imbalances, and might contribute to a finicky appetite.

In my opinion, the ideal age at which to select and introduce a puppy to its new home is seven weeks.

The puppy should receive its first immunization injection against the major infectious diseases when it reaches eight weeks of age, and should be treated for infestation with roundworms. Because these parasites spend a portion of their life cycles outside of the gastrointestinal tracts of the bitches, even the cleanest and best operated kennels cannot totally rid their breeding stock of the common roundworms. During late pregnancy, some of these worm larvae cross the placental membranes. Later, they may be transmitted in the bitch's milk. These worms migrate through the tissues of the puppies within a few weeks and eventually reach the stomach and intestines, where they mature. For this reason your veterinarian will ask you to submit a fresh stool specimen from your puppy on its first well-puppy visit. You should bring your new puppy to the family veterinarian soon after you obtain it. The fee is wisely spent if any major defects are revealed. If you wait too long, returning the puppy becomes enormously difficult.

How to Choose a Mature Mixed-bred Dog

There are some guidelines that will help you select a mature mixed-bred dog who will make a splendid companion for several years.

In contrast to selecting a young puppy in which early development of coordination and juvenile behavior are all-important, one places more emphasis upon the personality of the adult dog. If it tends to cower or is openly aggressive with strangers, you may be sure that it is demonstrating signs of psychological disturbances that probably will make it unsuitable as a companion.

Avoid a dog with obvious diseases or disorders. Once you have accepted the new dog into your family, your attachment will grow stronger with the passage of time; it will be much more difficult to separate yourself from the dog than it would be to reject it from the very beginning.

Obtaining a Mixed-bred Dog

Before you obtain the dog, have it examined by your veterinarian to certify that your choice is sound. Newly acquired adult dogs also should be examined for intestinal parasites and heartworms and should be vaccinated, if appropriate.

Costs of Purchase and Maintaining Health During the First Year of Life

Whereas the selling prices of high quality and desirable mixed-breed dogs vary widely across the United States, some averages can be calculated by comparing newspaper advertisements from various locales. In early 1988, a mixed-bred puppy cost between $5 to $75, depending upon whether the puppy is of a popular breed mixture such as York-shire terrier X poodle, cocker spaniel X poodle, schnauzer X poodle, Lhasa Apso X, or dachshund X. Of course, some exceptional animals command higher prices. Among these would be the many hunting hounds, pointers, setters, and retriever crosses.

Veterinary fees for routine multi-injection vaccinations and deworming, obedience training equipment, doggy utensils, and bedding will amount to another $100 to $250. In those regions where heartworms are prevalent, prophylactic medication would cost approximately $18 to $24 for the small dogs and about $35 to $50 for larger dogs. Food expenses vary widely with the products and the volume fed. There are some excellent new rations available, but they are more expensive than some other commercial products. Generally, they are worth their additional cost.

Supplies and Housing

Availability of Fresh Water

Along with a nutritious diet, dogs always must have ready access to clean fresh water in a suitable bowl. Domesticated dogs usually drink from standing water several times during the day. If they are fed dry food, their consumption of water will be correspondingly greater than if they are fed moist or semimoist diets. Wild (feral) dogs tend to drink less often, but lap up a greater volume at one time.

A broad-based, wide-mouthed container, or a ball-check automatic sipper device that attaches to water pipes outdoors may offer water. A bowl, when furnished, must be cleaned regularly because saliva and standing water provide a ready home to bacteria and fungi.

Examples of some types of food and water dishes for dogs. Each of these is unlikely to be easily upset and spill its contents.

Proper Toys

Playthings such as balls and bone-like objects are enjoyed by almost any dog even though they are not essential to a dog's intellectual development.

It is very important that any toys be large enough to prevent their being accidently swallowed or choked upon. Toys and balls should be made from nontoxic materials and should be sufficiently sturdy to survive frequent mauling. Large beef knuckle bones obtained from your butcher may be prized by your dog, but after your carpeting, upholstery, clothing, and dog have become messy with tallow and bone marrow remnants, you will rue the day you allowed your dog to gnaw on a real bone. Chicken, turkey, lamb, pork, or smaller beef bones also should be avoided because they may splinter and injure delicate soft tissues after they are swallowed by your dog. Rawhide bones or the hard-milled Nylabones are appropriate substitutes, and appear to be well accepted by even the most eager puppy who is teething.

You must be careful to keep stuffed toys with sewn-on eyes and the like away from your dog because they may be easily gnawed, pulled off, and swallowed, thus causing choking and or intestinal obstruction. If sharing its new home with a baby, your puppy must not be allowed to have access to nursing bottles and, especially, rubber nipples, for they can be accidentally swallowed and cause much trouble.

Rags, nylon hose, and similar stringy materials must be avoided, because they are readily swallowed and can produce serious, even fatal, damage to the tender gastrointestinal tracts of young dogs. Similarly, old shoes, belts, and other objects of apparel should not be offered as toys. If adornments and laces become detached and are swallowed, surgical intervention may be required. Some materials are toxic and others will block the passage of food and stools through the intestines.

Sleeping and Feeding Areas in the House

Dogs have definite preferences for sites where they rest and sleep. A minority of dogs prefer their owner's bed as their "nesting" place. In some instances, this arrangement can be defended but,

Supplies and Housing

Your dog should have its own bed in which to rest.

An Outdoor Run?

If gardens must be kept dog-free or if your living style does not permit regular leash-led walking exercise, an outdoor run might be considered. However, most dogs are very human-oriented, sensitive creatures and probably would eagerly choose closer contact with their owners than is afforded by a kennel and outdoor run environment.

An outdoor run, if it must be used, should have a sloping concrete surface that can be washed down daily and provision for the disposal of feces without creating a vermin hazard. Your dog's stools must be

When necessary, an outdoor run can be used to confine your dog.

generally, the dog should have its own bed. Hygienic considerations should rule out shared human-canine sleeping quarters—the cleaning bills will be reduced if your dog is not permitted to use your bed.

Most pet shops carry or can order wicker baskets that have been designed as dog beds. These are generally quite serviceable. However, young dogs sometimes chew wicker, producing fragments that would harm delicate tissues. A form-fitted mattress with a washable cloth cover is placed into the basket. Young puppies should be carried to their new bed each time you find them sleeping in some other place. Dogs are intelligent and will soon learn to use only the bed that you have provided.

Whatever you use for your dog's sleeping quarters, it is very important that it is situated in a draft-free place that is readily accessible to both you and your dog.

A small, freely-swinging "doggie door" should be installed if possible, so that your pet can go outside to eliminate whenever it wishes to do so. Whereas this arrangement is impossible in a high-rise apartment or condominium, it is very desirable in a ground-floor home with enclosed yard or run.

disposed of frequently and properly. Many commercial kennels employ heavy-duty garbage disposal units plumbed into the sewerage line for this purpose. The walls of the run area should be constructed from chain-link fencing so that your dog can see some of its surrounding world. No housing arrangement for an animal should be so sterile that boredom will lead to behavioral disturbances. Many veterinarians and professional dog handlers have observed that dogs kept in kennels generally are not as social as those allowed to live in the home environment with their owners.

So that your dog will have a comfortable place in which to retire and/or seek refuge from the elements, a doghouse or rain-tight, draft-free shelter should be provided. It should be designed with an airspace between its floor and the concrete surface with the floor fitted with durable padded carpeting. A removable roof or one that is hinged in the center so that both flaps can be raised; (see illustration at right) will facilitate cleaning the interior of the shelter. The doorway should be provided with a piece of heavy carpeting or similar material, hung from above, to prevent drafts. Some shade-providing overhang or foliage also should be present.

Fresh drinking water from a ready source is an absolute necessity. Self-actuated drinking devices are available from animal feed dealers and some pet shops. Because they can not be fouled with food or wastes, these low-pressure drinking fountains are ideal for kenneled dogs. In freezing weather, however, they can become inoperative.

Remember that even the best mannered canine will bark from time to time. Just as you have taken

A snug and draft free doghouse is necessary for the outdoor dog during inclement weather

steps to eliminate unpleasant odors and fly infestation, you must also make certain that your neighbors' rights to peace and quiet are respected. An outdoor run can be maintained in a socially acceptable fashion, but it takes a great deal of owner commitment.

Caring for Mixed-bred Dogs

Helping Your Puppy Get Started

Your new puppy will need your understanding and forbearance for the first few weeks after being separated from its mother and siblings, and introduced into the unfamiliar environment of your home.

The puppy is a naturally curious creature, ever eager to examine and sniff everything. Its new teeth are just beginning to push through the gums during this same time, and the desire to gnaw nearly everything within its new world often provokes the new owner.

Immediately show your puppy the site in your kitchen or utility room where it is convenient for you to place its food and water. The ravenous appetites of healthy puppies can be used to your advantage. At least for the first week or two, feed your dog the same food that it was being offered originally. In order to change the diet, do it gradually over a period of a week or two, starting with 90 percent original food and 10 percent new food. Increase the percentage of new food daily until the entire diet is composed of the new item(s). The gradual process of the human-animal bond and socialization will be well on its way once your puppy becomes accustomed to receiving its food from you.

Firmness and consistency are needed to train a dog. You must establish that your commands must be obeyed in order to assume your proper role as the dominant individual in the human-animal bonding process. If you corrected the puppy for a misdeed yesterday, you *must* use the same correction for that same infraction today and tomorrow. Nothing will confuse a young dog more than uncertainty about your reaction to its behavior.

For example, what should you to do when the new puppy whines when left alone in its bed at the time you retire for the evening? This whining is both predictable and perfectly normal. Before entering your home, the puppy had its mother and littermates to comfort and keep it occupied. Now it finds itself alone. You should go back to the basket, pet the puppy as you speak to it in soothing tones, but do not pick it up or allow it to follow you back to your bedroom. If your resolve wilts, your future relationship with your dog will surely be confused.

During the first few days after acquiring a young puppy, never leave it alone in your home. Because this is a critical time in the bonding and early training process, you must avoid allowing the puppy to feel it is being abandoned. If this happens, the puppy will give in to the urge to whine and bark incessantly. When this fails to bring you back, the puppy will usually begin to chew on any object in its grasp. The damage to your home during even a brief absence can be substantial. At this point, your anger will be directed toward the puppy and you will feel the anguish of defeat. During short absences and at night, the puppy can be confined to a large collapsible shipping crate that is lined by newspapers equipped with a bed and the puppy's food and water bowls. This will help establish a "home " and avoid accidents. Also, this arrangement can be set up in a friend's home when you travel with your dog or when you expect guests and wish to confine your pet during meals in another home.

Many people have found that if you place a metal wind-up* clock or portable, battery-powered radio tuned to music or human voices in the bed with a very young puppy as you prepare it for the evening, the dog tends to rest more quietly. There are many theories about this, but the technique works in most cases and is worth trying.

What Your New Puppy Must Learn Now

Puppies, even when very young, are capable of learning their names, elementary housebreaking

---

*Only a metal clock should be used, because even small puppies can totally destroy less durable timepieces. Similarly, only sturdy battery-powered radios should be used to prevent the possibility of accidental electrocution.

Caring for Mixed-bred Dogs

(see page 47), and even a few of the simple obedience commands.

Names for dogs should be no more than two syllables; ideally, the name should be monosyllabic. Each time you speak to the puppy, use its name in a normal conversational voice. Calling it by name will naturally lead to the command, "Come!" Reinforce each successful lesson by giving verbal praise and softly stroking the puppy's head, neck, shoulders, and chest when it obeys your order. Negative or improper responses to your commands should summon your firm and immediate "No!" Because it often only makes the new puppy fearful of you in particular, and humans in general, most obedience trainers avoid physical punishment.

Immediately upon being brought home, the new puppy should be fitted with a soft woven nylon training collar. The best collars are those fitted with a metal ring at each end. A soft, free-running loop is formed by placing one length of the collar into the ring at one end. The ring at the free end can then be attached to the snap-eye fastener at the end of the leather or nylon leash. (Do not use a metal chain leash.) Remember that although your puppy will grow very rapidly, the collar will remain the same size; you must check it every few days and adjust or replace it as soon as it becomes even slightly snug on the dog's neck. An alternative to the conventional training collar is the Halti head collar designed in England. It is a humane and very practical device that is fitted over the dog's muzzle and back of its neck, rather than encircling the animal's neck. It controls the head of the puppy without placing undue pressure on its tender neck.

Leash-naive puppies usually object strenuously the first few times that their collars are attached to a leash and their normally exuberant activities are curtailed. Leash training should be a gradual process, taking place over a span of one to two days. Once the puppy has become accustomed to wearing its soft collar, attach the lightweight leash, and while you watch to see that it does not become entangled on projecting objects, allow the puppy to drag its leash around for a few minutes at a time.

The well-mannered dog does not beg for food while its human companions are eating.

With verbal and gentle hand-stroking praise, again reinforce the puppy's good behavior. Within a very brief time, the puppy will be used to the feel of the collar and the weight of the leash.

The first time you take your new puppy outside to greet the world surrounding your home, walk only a few yards. Remember that the tiny puppy has to take many more steps to equal one of your strides. If every brief outing is successful and pleasurable for the two of you, both of you will soon look forward to leash-controlled walks.

Infringing on your meals by begging for snacks and handouts is a behavioral trait that is distasteful to many people. The habit of allowing puppies to beg food from the table often leads to their refusal to accept commercially prepared dog food in favor of more tasty "people" food, to nutritional imbalances, and to canine obesity. Discourage begging by merely refusing even the most appealing whines and attempts to gain your attention. A firm "no!" and a forced return of the offending puppy to its sleeping basket or to another site away from your immediate presence will usually convey your message of disapproval.

Table scraps, if fed to your dog, should be trimmed of excess fat. They should be mixed with the dog's regular food in such a fashion to only partially flavor the commercial food, but not take its place.

Basic Grooming

Bathing

Puppies do not have to reach some minimal age before their first bath. So, like human infants, they should be bathed when they become soiled. The bath water should be warm, and mild soap or infant shampoo will clean the fur. Protect delicate occular tissues from soap or shampoo irritation by instilling a drop or two of mineral oil into each eye. Any food residue and fecal material should be carefully softened and removed. Thoroughly rinse the soap and carefully dry the coat with absorptive cotton toweling. If you think that it is required, a hand-held hair dryer, set on a moderate heat, can be used to complete the drying and to fluff the fur. Do not direct the warm air from the dryer toward the eyes and do not leave the dryer unattended where the puppy can chew on its power cord and be electrocuted.

Your dog's coat, between baths, should be regularly brushed, and its eyebrows, mustaches, and chin whiskers gently combed to free them from tangles. Start your dog's grooming gently and at an early age and it will come to enjoy these attentions. If you wait until the dog is already filthy and its coat a mass of tangled knots, the grooming experience will be unpleasant for both of you and probably should be accomplished by a professional dog groomer.

Some examples of grooming instruments that can be used to maintain your dog's coat and claws.

Care of the Claws and Pads

Claws: Most dogs have eighteen claws when they are born: five on each forefoot and four on each hind foot. The first, or dew-claw, corresponding to the human thumb, is set above the surface upon which a dog's foot makes contact when it walks. Because of this location, the dewclaws tend to grow around and inward, like a ram's horn, unless they are periodically shortened. By running on rough and uneven surfaces, the dog wears down its claws, but carpeting and soft grass lawns do not provide much abrasion. Under these conditions the claws will grow too long and may curl inward toward soft toe pads, thus injuring them. Therefore, the claws should be clipped whenever necessary.

The canine claw, like human fingernails and toenails, grows outward in an ever-lengthening process from a germinal bed rich in blood vessels. If the claw is cut off too short, it will bleed and cause pain to the dog. Go slowly and trim off only thin slices with the clipper; this will keep you from removing too much and establish confidence in

Caring for Mixed-bred Dogs

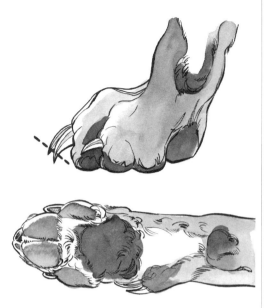

Generally, only the tips of your dog's claws need to be clipped. If they are overgrown, they may have to be shortened by a professional. Your dog's soft foot pads are very sensitive organs that are easily lacerated.

your dog. In time it will learn that it can trust you to trim these very sensitive appendages.

A specialized instrument such as the Resco or White's nail clipper is the proper device with which to keep the claws trimmed. Both are inexpensive and are available from pet shops.

Pads: The dog's soft, leathery digital and foot pads usually do not require special care to maintain them in health. They may, however, be abraded by running on rough surfaces if the feet have not been "toughened" gradually. Also the pads may be burned on hot surfaces, penetrated by sharp thorns, wood and metal slivers, and may be cut by shards of broken glass and other objects. You should examine the pads and the spaces between the pads carefully for the presence of cuts, abrasions, or foreign

bodies if your puppy or adult dog suddenly becomes lame and refuses to put weight on one of its feet.

After treating the abrasion, laceration, or wound to prevent infection, or removing the offending foreign object, the foot may require bandaging to keep the injured part protected from further trauma or contamination and to greatly diminish the pain.

Care of the Ears

The ear canals on the outside of the eardrums secrete earwax, called cerumen, which is an entirely normal and essential process. You should not interfere with your dog's ears unless you are directed by your family veterinarian to treat them. Do not routinely insert cotton-tipped applicators to clean the inside. It is not necessary, and may only cause problems by compressing the earwax into the narrow portions of the canal and/or pushing foreign bodies deeply against the eardrum.

If your veterinarian suggests that your dog's ears be cleaned, it is usually wise for it to be done professionally by those who possess the experience and equipment.

Dogs, unlike cats, rarely harbor parasitic ear mites. But, if found, they are readily eliminated by any of several prescriptions that will be dispensed by your veterinarian.

Ear ticks, *Otobius megnini*, are most often found outdoors, but once established in a dog's ear(s), they can become chronic. Ear ticks are best removed by your veterinarian, who will use an illuminated otoscope to see them and a special long-jawed forceps to grasp and remove them from the deeper portions of the ear canals.

Make certain that you are properly instructed on how to apply any prescribed ear medications dispensed by your veterinarian so that they will be effective for your dog. Generally, a small amount of the liquid preparation is placed into the affected ear canal(s) and is massaged down into the deeper regions by gentle manipulation of the lower portions of the ear flap, or pinna. A piece of cleansing tissue placed over your index finger will remove

Caring for Mixed-bred Dogs

Your dog's ears should be examined routinely for the presence of foreign objects.

excess fluid and any exudate loosened from the lining of the ear canal.

Some mixed-bred dogs are characterized by excessively hairy ear canals. Often professional dog groomers remove this hair as part of the grooming process, but this is often unnecessary and only encourages ear inflammation later. This hair has evolved as a protection against foreign body entrance into the ear canals and does not interfere with your dog's hearing.

Care of the Eyes

You should not be burdened by having to give special care to your pet's eyes, except for routinely cleaning any mucus or foreign matter from its eyelids. Occasionally a dog's eyelashes may grow inward, rather than outward, or it may possess an extra row of eyelashes along one or both eyelids. These extra lashes can be removed by electrolysis or by relatively minor eyelid surgery.

During times of pollen release by certain plants, or in extremely dusty environments, any of the nonprescription ophthalmic irrigating solutions

available at any pet shop or pharmacy can be used for your dog. An excellent example of such a product is Dacriose Solution. In an emergency, if a noxious substance irritates the eye and lid tissues, flush the eye with warm water, a mild salt solution using 1 to 1½ teaspoons table salt to a pint of warm water, or nontrimerasol containing contact lens soaking solution. Hard contact lens solutions are buffered to resemble the chemical environment of the eye and contain methylcellulose as a wetting agent, which makes these solutions an excellent artificial tear source. Packaged in soft plastic containers that make their use in rinsing the eyes very

You can inspect your dog's eyes by depressing the lower eyelids with your thumb or finger. This will allow you to see any foreign matter or objects.

easy, these solutions can be instilled by holding the eyelids open with one hand and with the other hand directing a gentle stream. To avoid contamination, do not allow the tip of the bottle to touch the lid or eye tissues.

Care of Teeth

Teeth and gums played a major role in dogs' daily routine over the millions of years they evolved from more primitive mammals. The large paired upper and lower canine teeth were used to attack the

25

prey upon which the animals subsisted and also to protect them from other predatory species that would, as a link in the food chain, prey upon them. The prey was torn into pieces small enough to be swallowed by the incisor teeth. The large, shearing molars were used to cut tendons and other tough resilient tissues.

Soft diets tend to foster the accumulation of soft dental plaque which, if not removed, turns to stony tartar, called *calculus*. This accumulation of tartar is soon accompanied by gingivitis, or gum inflammation. Once the gums become chronically inflamed, bacteria can gain ready access to the vascular system and often are carried with the circulating blood to the heart, where they infect the heart valves, which are essential to directing the blood from the lungs and into the aorta. Bacteria originating on the teeth also may infect the kidneys, joints, and other sites thoughout the body.

Include hard-baked dog biscuits and kibbled dog food in the diet. You may wish to offer an occasional well-cooked and degreased veal or beef bone in the routine diet to keep your dog's teeth clean. It is not advisable to allow your dog to chew such large bones daily, but rather, once every two or three weeks, and then only for a day or two at the most. If substantial amounts of bone are swallowed, it may cause constipation; if offered too often, hard bones will cause abnormal and excessive tooth enamel wear, thus shortening and weakening the teeth. Some authorities advise substituting defatted oxtails for the regular diet once every seven to ten days.

Open your dog's mouth once weekly and inspect the gums, teeth, tongue, and lips. After approaching the dog and speaking in soothing tones, gently open its mouth by holding its upper jaw with one hand and, using the fingers of your other hand, depress the lower jaw. Open the mouth only enough to permit you to see the interior. A source of light coming over your shoulder will help illuminate the structures you wish to see. Keep the mouth open only long enough to complete your inspection and, after you have finished, give praise for your

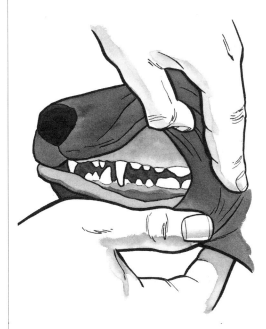

Your dog's teeth and gums should be inspected regularly.

companion's cooperation.

Canine toothpastes are now available. Once your dog becomes used to having its teeth cleaned, this activity becomes part of its daily routine. Your veterinarian can remove any already accumulated plaque or tartar after your dog has been mildly sedated or anesthetized with a short-duration anesthetic agent. With the newer chemical restraint and anesthetic products and techniques available today, the risk of anesthesia is minimized.

Mixed-bred dogs are notable for their intelligence. Even the youngest puppy can be taught to *sit*. slightly older dogs can also be taught to *stay* and to *come* on command.

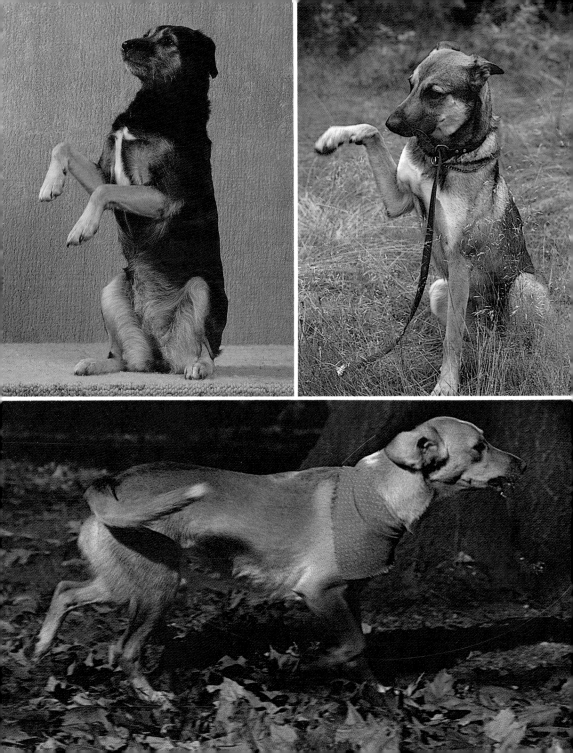

Caring for Mixed-bred Dogs

Appropriate veterinary dental therapy often may salvage cracked, chipped, or broken teeth. Even endodontic procedures (root canal treatments) are a sensible alternative to extraction in companion animals. These dental techniques are becoming standard practice in progressive veterinary practices.

Badly diseased or abscessed teeth should not be ignored, because they can be a source of chronic infection that may soon extend to other (nondental) structures or organs. They must be extracted by your veterinarian and the few dollars spent to correct dental disease often will not only save you much greater medical expenses later but will, almost undoubtedly, permit your dog to live a longer, healthier life.

Other tricks that clever mutts often take in stride include *sit up* (sometimes called *beg*), *shake* or *paw*, and *fetch*— a game that owners generally tire of long before their canine companions.

Daily Life with a Mixed-bred Dog

Lifting and Carrying the Dog

The correct way to pick up a puppy is by placing one hand around and beneath its chest, right in front of its forelimbs, and supporting the rear quarters with the other hand. Be gentle when picking up the puppy; remember how you feel when an elevator rises too rapidly for your comfort. Whereas the puppy's dam may have picked it up by the scruff of the neck, the puppy is now older and heavier; if you employ this method, you probably will cause discomfort, if not outright pain. Depending upon its size, an older dog is best picked up by placing one hand or arm in front of the forelimbs and the other behind the rear limbs and lifting straight up in one steady movement. It is useful sometimes to hold the two front legs together between the thumb and middle fingers of one hand because this maneuver helps steady the limbs and keeps the dog from struggling.

Pick up injured dogs very carefully so that 1) you will not cause additional pain, and 2) you can avoid causing the dog to injure you if it attempts to protect itself. In most cases it is prudent to apply a soft gauze or cloth-strip binding around the injured dog's muzzle, cinching it just in front of the eyes. Several wraps of cloth are placed over and around the muzzle, tying the last two on top of the neck. The last tie should be a bow knot so that it may be released easily, when appropriate.

If you suspect a back injury, the dog should be placed very gently upon a solid, unyielding object, such as a wide board or small door, which can serve as a litter.

A puppy must always be properly supported when being lifted. Place one hand against the rib cage and the other under the puppy's rear end.

Dogs and Children

Crossbred dogs have been recognized for many years as suitable companions for children. It was not until about three hundred years ago that serious line- and/or inbreeding began to be practiced to develop dogs with specific physical and behavioral characteristics. Even though most dogs possess native intelligence, responsiveness to the wishes of their human companions, and loyalty, there is no guarantee that all dogs will immediately exhibit fondness for every child they encounter. Several of our own dogs were amazingly not only tolerant of children, but displayed what can only be termed genuine affection for youngsters. One of our male dogs would, however, bark and growl menacingly at the approach of all persons wearing uniforms, even those he spied in adjacent automobiles as we drove in our car. Because we had obtained him as an adult animal, we could only speculate that he must have been threatened or abused by someone dressed in a uniform.

We have always brought our dogs aboard our houseboat over the years as we plied the waters of the Sacramento-San Joaquin River delta system, and each has proven herself a very seaworthy member of our crew. Our Yorkshire terrier/poodle mix and miniature schnauzer/poodle cross were particularly sensitive to the high-pitched piping voices of small children, even though these dogs had been brought up with small children. The voices of some small children may be an irritant to some dogs. Unfortunately some children will tease a dog to the point where the animal's patience is exhausted and it seeks to protect itself from further torment by aggressive behavior.

Because of their outbred heritage, which often enhances physical vigor and intelligence, most crossbred dogs naturally make splendid watch-dogs. This trait can create a situation at times where a child might, by its actions, cause a dog to act in a manner that could result in injury to the youngster. Disturbing *any* dog while it is eating is unwise, and children should be cautioned about this. Allow the child to remove the dog's food and water bowls after the dog has finished using them. A child can be taught how to brush a dog gently and do other simple tasks that will help instill confidence in both the child and dog.

When your dog is on a leash outside of your home or is in your automobile, it may be approached by strangers who wish to pet it. This is only natural, but it is important that the dog be allowed to sniff the back of the hand of the person and be given the opportunity to react before actual hand contact is made with it. This also affords the person time to withdraw the proffered hand in case the dog does not wish to be touched. This is particularly important in the case of exuberant young children who are unaware of how to approach a strange dog. A ball or other plaything carelessly tossed over an intervening backyard wall and re-trieved without the knowledge of the household's resident(s) might trigger a defensive action by the dog, who is only protecting the property of its owner. Restrain your dog when a stranger arrives at the door of your home, so that it will not act impulsively.

To protect both child and dog from accidents, never leave very young children unattended with a dog. Once an older child has demonstrated that it knows how to treat your dog with respect and the dog has reacted positively to that child, they may be left to play together from time to time. Even in such cases, however, but adult supervision should be close by in case it is required.

Dogs and a New Baby

Your dog should be introduced to the baby as soon as possible, under most circumstances. Remember, the dog may have been a surrogate "only child" before the birth of the new baby, and it is only natural for the dog to express some jealousy if, after arriving home with an infant, you totally ignore the presence of your canine companion. It is a good idea to allow your dog to see and sniff the scent of the baby, but not lick it. While making this introduction, make certain that you praise the dog and tell it how good a beastie it is. If you follow these simple steps, dogs will almost invariably bond with the newest addition to their "pack" and begin to demonstrate not only great interest and devotion, but also an immediate tendency to guard the baby and to shield it from any perceived threat from outside your household.

Before the anticipated arrival of your new baby, it is wise to have your dog's stools microscopically examined for parasitic worm ova and protozoa, which can be transmitted from dogs to humans. Periodic reexaminations are also advisable.

Many of us have grown up with at least one dog in our family, and we appear to have been well served psychologically from our early experiences!

Daily Life with a Mixed-bred Dog

Dogs and Other Pets

Dog's naturally show intense interest in other animals; some will bond strongly to other dogs, cats, even hamsters, guinea pigs, rabbits, mice, rats, and birds. Remember, though, that some of these other animals were the natural prey for the dog's ancient ancestors. There can be no definite statement or guarantee that a given dog will accept another animal (or, for that matter, another human) as a friend. The most important concept is that the initial introduction can be all-important to the future relationship. It is vital to make the introduction to another new animal, just as with a new baby in the family, positive for the resident dog. Show it how much you care for it by saying your dog's name and petting it while handling the new animal. Allow it to see and smell the newcomer and, if appropriate, even lick it.

Dogs can be introduced easily to kittens, and adult cats often adopt new puppies without too much fuss. It is only when both the dog and the cat are adults when first introduced to each other that problems arise.

If your dog prefers to eat your cat's food, you need only place the cat's food dish on a high place where the cat can reach it, but the dog cannot. Commercial cat food often contains a higher protein level than is necessary for dogs, therefore its consumption by your dog should be discouraged. A similar situation can develop if your dog becomes accustomed to eating table scraps. Your dog just might develop a preference for these items, refusing to eat dog food.

A Second Dog?

There are no compelling reasons, in my opinion, for not having two dogs in the same household. If there were, I would be guilty of hypocrisy, because we have had as many as three dogs at one time. The *timing* of the acquisition of a second dog is of great importance. Puppies readily learn good and bad habits from their older siblings or peers, just as children do. It is for this reason that it usually is better to bring a puppy into a home in which there is already a relatively mature dog. The early training of the new animal will be easier as it observes the behavior of its older canine tutor. This is particularly true with respect to housebreaking and obedience training.

The first of our dogs to learn to swim to our boat, then climb straight up a vertical four-step boarding ladder, was our Yorkshire terrier-poodle mix, Shibui (Japanese for *understated elegance*). Within a day or two she had taught, by example, our miniature schnauzer/poodle cross, Raisin, to mimic her behavior. Soon their example had been copied by our third dog, Molly, a noble mongrel of dubious ancestry. Before long, people would wade to our boat, timidly knock on the hull, and ask to see the dogs who were becoming famous because they routinely "jumped ship", swam ashore to relieve themselves, then swam back to the houseboat, climbed the ladder, and hopped back aboard. Soon these dogs were the subjects of videotapes depicting "smart" dog tricks! Alas, we cannot take credit for this show of obvious canine cleverness, because one of our dogs had discovered independently that a boat's boarding ladder was no impediment to returning "home."

When first introducing the new puppy to an older resident dog, it is vital to avoid instilling a feeling of jealousy or partiality. As when introducing a new baby to a resident dog, make certain to praise the older dog so it knows it is being noticed at the same time that so much attention is being given to the newcomer.

Take time to give the older dog a snack of dry kibble or puppy chow when feeding the puppy. Unless the older dog has kidney or heart disease, puppy food will do no harm. The few extra calories will, for a week or so, be expended in the extra exercise playing with the puppy. As a general rule, follow the directions on the container of puppy food with respect to the amount and frequency of feeding. The two dogs should be fed from separate dishes, but they may share the same water bowl and sleeping quarters. In fact, by allowing the two dogs to sleep together, you will avoid the problem of the new puppy wanting to follow you into your bedroom instead of sleeping in its own bed.

Like infants, puppies are stimulated to urinate and defecate shortly after they eat. Because they are immature, their ability to retain a full urinary bladder and colon is limited in comparison to a grown dog, therefore, it is important to take the puppy out for a leash-controlled walk soon after it has eaten. The older dog also should be taken out, even if it does not have to eliminate. With one leashed dog on either side of you, a routine of businesslike behavior soon will be established, and so these communal walks will result in almost immediate productivity, rather than sight-seeing excursions. Take the young puppy out in the evening for its last exercise and give it the opportunity to relieve itself just before being put to bed. This will help train it to retain its wastes throughout the night.

Mild conflicts may naturally arise between any two animals, and occasionally a younger animal, as it grows to adulthood, will gain dominance. At first, this elevated rank may manifest itself in the selection of favored toys, food, sleeping arrangements, and during aggressive play. When playing with the dogs together, try to fairly give each dog its equal share of your attention.

Travel by Automobile, Train, and Air

Coping with and Preventing Motion Sickness

Having vacationed for years with our own dogs aboard our houseboat, I can heartily champion the inclusion of the family dog(s) in those vacation plans in which a canine companion would represent a bonus rather than a burden.

Inexperienced canine travelers, like their human counterparts, must gradually develop a tolerance of motion. The easiest way to condition a dog to motion is to take it on very brief trips of only a few blocks, gradually lengthening trips to several miles as the dog develops a tolerance. When starting this training, schedule the outing before feeding time.

Vocally praise your dog for being a fine companion. Attach the dog's leash to its collar so that there will be a natural association with a forthcoming outing.

Motion sickness has warning signs and does not suddenly manifest itself by immediate explosive vomiting. One of the first signs of threatening nausea is salivation and frequent swallowing movements. At the first evidence of this behavior, you should immediately park your car and allow the dog to get out and walk around with its leash on. Only a few minutes are required usually to reestablish the middle ear's equilibrium and settle the dog's queasiness. As soon as your dog seems to be normal again, place it back into your car and drive until signs of early nausea return. Repeat this process over and over and, within a few days, even a very young dog will become a seasoned traveler. It is but a minor step to travel by train and airplane once your dog is accustomed to automobile trips. After dogs overcome their initial motion sickness, they eagerly anticipate each opportunity to go for rides—unless these trips are only to the veterinarian's office!

Canine travelers, even the experienced, seem to fare better if fed at the end of the trip, rather than just before departure.

If you must take a trip with your dog before it has been conditioned to travel, it may be given medication to reduce its sensitivity to motion. Nonprescription drugs such as Dramamine, Bonamine, or Bonadexine will, in very small dosages, yield excellent results. They are relatively safe, but in high dosages will induce sleepiness and an inability of a dog to regulate its body temperature. These drugs should not be given to pregnant bitches. Generally ⅛ to ¼ of a small child's dosage is sufficient to inhibit motion sickness in a small dog. Adult large dogs will require as much as ½ to a full tablet. Your family veterinarian can prescribe or dispense mild tranquilizer tablets that will help prevent motion sickness.

Antimotion sickness medications ideally should be given at least one hour before the anticipated departure time. As an alternative to medication for preventing motion sickness, you can give your dog one or more small capsules of dried ground gingerroot. Available at health food stores, this common herb has shown promise as an antimotion sickness agent with the advantage of not inducing drowsiness. The dosage is not critical because any excess will be metabolized as a nutrient.

Shipping crates come in many types and sizes.

When anticipating travel aboard a train or commercial airplane, be certain to inquire from the carrier what arrangements and rules must be followed. Often, a very small dog will be permitted to travel in the passenger cabin with you. Larger dogs will have to be transported in the baggage compartment. Your dog probably will be confined to an approved shipping crate. As is the case with automobile travel, food should be withheld before departure. Water can be offered until approximately one hour before the dog must be crated. A leashed walk will encourage your dog to empty its urinary bladder and bowels.

Arrangements should be made on prolonged flights for your dog to be taken from its crate, exercised on a lead, and given water. Allowing your dog to walk and stretch its muscles and joints every few hours is important to its health.

Items to be Included in the Luggage

If veterinary prescription medications are being given to your dog, it is imperative that you pack a supply to last the entire length of the trip; it might be difficult to refill prescriptions away from home. It is advisable to carry a copy of your dog's rabies vaccination and/or health certificate, issued by your veterinarian, when you are traveling away from home with your pet. A container of a nonprescription antidiarrhea medication is a welcome addition to the kit. Constipation is an unusual problem, but if your traveling dog experiences difficulty in defecation, a small amount of milk of magnesia (⅛ to ½ of a child's dose, depending upon the weight of your dog) usually brings relief. A container of antiflea and tick spray or powder should be considered if your itinerary will take you where an infestation is likely.

You may have to pack a supply of your dog's regular dog food, an appropriate food dish, and water bowl. If you are traveling by automobile, a plastic bottle of water will free you from having to locate a source of uncontaminated water. A warm blanket or washable heavy cotton bath towel, your dog's leash, and grooming utensils also should be packed.

First aid supplies suitable for human use are appropriate for emergency veterinary care, in case of accident.

Travel Abroad

Securing the Appropriate Travel Documentation

Special documentation may be necessary if you travel abroad with your dog. Also check with the consulate or embassy of each nation whose territory you will travel through to obtain permits for animal transit. These permits, based upon a standard health examination and certification that your dog is not harboring infectious disease, generally expire after 31 days and may have to be renewed by one or more foreign veterinary inspectors. A complete set of your dog's health records that document vaccinations is essential. In most instances, booster injections should be administered two to three weeks before your anticipated departure.

Some countries insist upon a prolonged quarantine period which could be as long as six months. This quarantine is at your expense, and you will not be allowed to take your dog out of the quarantine facility until the full prescribed period has expired. You should know from the beginning of your travel planning that you will not have any right of appeal of these regulations.

Breeding

The Estrous Cycle

Two periods of potential reproductive activity per year are experienced by most sexually mature female dogs. Some bitches may go through only one annual cycle; others may have as many as three.

Normal canine estrous cycle stages are called, in sequence, *proestrus, estrus, metestrus* (or, if conception has occurred, *pregnancy*) and, finally, *anestrus*.

Proestrus is a preparatory phase of the cycle. Eggs are maturing within the ovaries, the lining of the uterus becomes more vascular and thickened, and finally a blood-tinged discharge comes from the vagina. The external genitalia of the bitch, called the vulva, become swollen to perhaps twice normal size. This phase lasts four to thirteen days; average length is nine days. Proestrus in the bitch is not equivalent to menstruation in humans, although there are some superficial similarities. During this period, male dogs will be attracted to the bitch by the discharge, but she usually will not allow them to mount and breed her.

The transition from proestrus to estrus is rather subtle. The vulva remains enlarged and the vaginal discharge becomes less blood-tinged until it is entirely clear and resembles thin mucus.

A yellowish discharge, which sometimes occurs, is not a reason for concern unless it becomes copious or continues for more than two weeks. Male dogs are even more avidly drawn to the bitch at this time, and most often she will allow males to mount and mate with her. As the eggs mature, the ovaries increase their estrogen secretions. The actual release of ripe eggs from the ovaries into the oviducts and eventually into the uterus occurs some time between the ninth to the fourteenth day after the very first sign of proestrus. Estrus continues for about nine to thirteen days. Although the bitch may remain receptive to males throughout the full time of estrus, the mature, released eggs are capable of being fertilized by sperm for only about four to six days.

If fertilization occurs, ovarian secretion of progesterone continues and the uterus remains receptive to the implantation and development of fertilized eggs. Six to ten days after ovulation the fertilized eggs reach the uterine "horns." Here they become partially imbedded in the uterine walls, which are richly supplied with blood vessels. Here the newly fertilized eggs develop into embryos and, later, fetuses.

If conception does not occur, the uterus enters another stage where it gradually becomes less vascular and relatively inactive. The ovarian hormone secretion changes from mostly estrogen to mostly progesterone.

Metestrus lasts about two months. During this phase, the mammary glands are prepared to secrete milk. Sometimes nonpregnant bitches will exhibit swelling of their breast tissues and nipples. Both pregnant and nonpregnant bitches may construct nests at this time and they may show their strong maternal instincts by carrying objects such as socks into these nests. They may even appear to nuzzle and try to nurse them, as if they were puppies. A slight sticky discharge may be noticed seeping from the nipples at this time. Metestrus usually lasts from 80 to 90 days following the initiation of proestrus.

Anestrus is the last phase of the estrous cycle. It begins at the close of metestrus and is a period of inactivity. The uterus shrinks markedly during this time and the ovaries are quiescent. Anestrus persists for approximately two to four months in most bitches, but this interval is quite variable. If pregnancy and nursing have continued to completion, anestrus will be delayed for their duration.

Chlorophyll tablets are available that, when given to bitches very early in their proestrus, will greatly diminish the sexually attractive odor of her vaginal discharges. As mentioned earlier, these tablets are *not* contraceptives.

I do not recommend the use of hormone injections and tablets, available from some veterinarians, that will postpone the onset of proestrus and estrus in bitches. These carry with them a significant risk of hormonal imbalance, uterine infections, and eventual sterility.

If you do not wish to breed your bitch at this time, you have several alternatives to having every sexually mature male dog in the neighborhood camp on your doorstep. Often the chlorophyll tablets will be all that is necessary to keep your bitch from becoming irresistible to eager suitors. A pair of protective panties that contain a pocket for holding a changeable absorptive pad may be purchased or constructed at home. If you have to, physically separate your bitch from your home until she is no longer so attractive to males by placing her in a boarding kennel for a week or so.

If your bitch is accidentally bred to a dog which, for any number of reasons, is unsuitable, your veterinarian can administer injections that will prevent implantation of the fertilized eggs. Often these injections will greatly accentuate the signs of estrus, but even if she is bred again within a few days, she is very unlikely to conceive. Note: these injections do carry with them some risk of uterine infection and anemia.

Breeding should be considered carefully, because of the great effort and time that it takes to properly care for a bitch and her puppies. The major upset to a household that occurs with the end of gestation and eventual delivery and care for a litter of demanding puppies can be substantial. Literally thousands of unwanted puppies and adult dogs are destroyed every day because of a gross imbalance between an oversupply and inadequate demand. No one wishes to worsen this situation by producing yet more puppies, no matter how appealing the idea seems to be at first.

If You Choose to Breed Your Bitch

Prior to being bred, your bitch should be given a thorough physical examination by your family veterinarian. Her immunizations must be current or be brought up to date, and she should be checked for internal parasites. A negative stool specimen does not necessarily denote the absence of worms. Most veterinarians and experienced breeders will generally de-worm the bitch even if evidence of worms is lacking.

Your bitch can be introduced to her prospective mate on about the ninth day of proestrus. It is almost invariably better to bring the bitch to the residence of the male. An experienced stud male will know what is expected of him and will take charge of the situation. The fewer human distractions, the better.

During copulation, a portion of the male's penis called the *bulbus glandus* becomes markedly engorged and the two animals remain "locked" together. This is entirely normal and no attempt should be made to separate the pair by spraying them with water or by other means. After a period of from ten to twenty minutes the male will dismount and he will eventually lose his erection. The pair should be left undisturbed for a while longer because they may copulate again.

If no mating occurs after the initial introduction, your bitch may not be quite ready and you should try pairing the two dogs again during the next day or two. Most professional breeders prefer to mate a pair of dogs at least twice during a given estrus period.

After about four weeks, a bitch that has conceived will show evidence of her pregnancy. Her abdomen will gradually enlarge and her mammary glands will become slightly swollen. As the fetuses grow larger, her abdomen becomes markedly distended. By the beginning of the ninth week of gestation, her breast tissue has greatly enlarged and the nipples are much longer than they were before mating. A small amount of milk may leak from the ends of the nipples, but you must not attempt to express milk by squeezing. During the first two days after delivery, colostrum, a special milk is secreted. It is rich in antibodies that the new puppies can absorb from their digestive tracts during the first day or two. By this mechanism, the puppies

Breeding

acquire their first immunity to those infectious diseases that the bitch was exposed to or vaccinated against. This is why it is so important that your bitch receive her booster injections before being bred. Because of the potential for inducing birth defects in the embryos during their early development, it is not recommended that pregnant bitches be vaccinated during the first two thirds of gestation. Beyond the first two days after birth, the puppies are no longer able to absorb colostrum, and it is soon replaced by normal milk. Although bitches' milk does not contain antibodies, it is rich in vitamins, minerals, protein, and calories.

Provide a whelping box of wicker, wood, or cardboard for your expectant bitch. An opening located a few inches above the bottom will readily admit the adult, but prevent the pups from tumbling out. Place a layer of freshly cleaned absorptive cotton toweling, without any unraveled threads, in the box. The best location for the box is a secluded draft-free corner of a quiet room. Some bitches do not seem to mind full exposure of their whelping quarters and brand new puppies, while others may be inhibited from behaving normally under the same circumstances. Try to be patient and understanding. Some bitches may display aggression toward others in the household during the first novel days of motherhood. You should place the bitch in the whelping box repeatedly, if she does not voluntarily adopt it, until she accepts it as the place that you have chosen for her.

The normal gestation period for canines is 63 days, plus or minus two or three days. Your family veterinarian may recommend that you bring your expectant bitch in for one last examination a few days prior to the expected delivery. At this time, the placement of the fetuses can be determined by a gentle pelvic examination.

The bitch should always have a source of fresh water placed conveniently close to her whelping box; she may, however, refuse food during the last 24 hours before delivery.

Become accustomed to obtaining your bitch's

A proper whelping box should be provided for the bitch and her new puppies.

rectal temperature once or twice daily, and plot it on a chart. You will find that your bitch's basal temperature will be between 100.5 and 102.5 degrees Fahrenheit. On the day that she will deliver her puppies, your bitch's rectal temperature will drop to below 100 degrees F. This is a good indication that the event for which you have been so anxiously awaiting is about to occur.

The Birth of Puppies

Actual labor may require several hours, especially for a bitch that has never whelped before. When your bitch is in labor, you will be able to see sequential waves of abdominal contractions. Even though they may be experiencing discomfort at this time, most bitches will not vocalize.

Delivery may be head first or rump first. It is beneficial if the first puppy is delivered head first, so that its muzzle can serve as a wedge to help dilate the cervical canal and pelvis. The placental fluids also will aid in this dilation process and in lubricating the birth canal. The puppies may be delivered within only a few minutes of each other, or they may be separated by an hour or more, during which time the bitch may rest, walk around and drink water. If, after straining for approximately forty-five minutes, your bitch has not delivered any puppies, you should call your veterinarian.

The placental membranes covering the muzzle of each puppy as it is delivered from the birth canal, will be removed by vigorous licking by the bitch. She will gently nuzzle the puppies to encourage them to move and eventually to nurse from her full nipples.

Occasionally a bitch will totally ignore her puppies. If she lacks normal maternal instincts, it will be up to you, as acting midwife, to attend to the puppies. A clean piece of cotton toweling should be used to cleanse the placental membranes from the puppies and to rub them in order to stimulate them to breathe and vocalize. Hopefully, the unattentive bitch will eventually accept and care for them. If she is not caring for them, it is vitally important to keep the puppies warm. They should be kept at least 96 degrees F. Warm water bottles and/or illumination may be used to supplement warmth. Heating pads may produce too much warmth.

Just before she eats the membranes, the umbilical cords, which were the only vascular connections between the dam and her puppies, are torn by the bitch; this is entirely normal. If she fails to do this, you will have to cut the cords yourself by using your clean fingers to pinch about two inches beneath the point where the cord attaches to the belly. A ligature made from stout thread or dental floss tied just above the site at which you will cut the cord will prevent blood loss if the umbilical vessels do not shrink spontaneously. A swab with Merthiolate or povidone iodine solution will help avoid navel infections. The remnants of the cord will soon dry and wither. After a few days, they will drop off entirely, leaving a tiny flat scar at the site of their former attachment.

Puppies' eyes are tightly closed and their ear flaps are carried flat against their heads when they are born. Usually, within 10 to 14 days, the puppies' eyes will open and their ears will begin to stand away from their head.

A typical litter contains four to six pups, but this may vary widely. Smaller dogs generally have correspondlingly small litters.

During the first two to three weeks, your bitch will care for her puppies. You need do nothing more than see to it that she is well watered and fed a ration that is formulated for puppies and/or nursing bitches and that her whelping blankets are changed as they become soiled. The bitch may have a greenish vaginal discharge for two to three weeks after delivering her puppies. This discharge, called *lochia*, is not a cause for concern.

Puppies begin to explore the world about them when they are three weeks old, using first their sense of smell, then those of sight, hearing, taste, and touch. It is your responsibility to remove from reach any toxic or otherwise hazardous materials. At this stage in their young lives, puppies test everything first by tasting and often by biting and chewing. A plugged-in electric cord, toxic houseplants, or household cleaning chemicals left within reach might prove fatal.

False Pregnancy: Explanation and Solutions

False pregnancy can occur in any mature female animal. It is not that uncommon in women and may be the reason for some cases of child abduction. In both women and dogs affected with this disorder, the physiologic disturbances are accompanied by serious psychological abnormalities.

Causes for this disorder include ovarian cysts and associated ovarian hormone dysfunction and pituitary hormone imbalances.

The most extreme signs of false pregnancy typically coincide with the actual time that a real pregnancy would terminate: about nine weeks after the previous start of proestrus.

Affected bitches may exhibit abdominal distention, mammary gland swelling and engorgement, and even actual lactation—many of the outward physical signs of a normal pregnancy. When seen in its most severe form, there even may be uterine or other abdominal contractions that mimic true labor. A nest is selected and household objects like socks or toys are carried into the nest, nuzzled as surrogate puppies, and aggressively protected.

Most cases of pseudopregnancy will resolve spontaneously but a proportion of affected bitches will eventually develop a condition called *pyometritis* and/or *pyometra*, depending upon subsequent events and will require far more aggressive treatment. The uterus becomes severely inflamed, and may, if the cervix remains closed, fill with pus. Often, intense thirst and increased urine output accompanies pyometra. This is a most serious condition that may require surgical removal of the ovaries and uterus, and although this is a form of

"spay," it is far more difficult than a routine sterilization operation and carries greater risk to the bitch. Also, it commands a much higher veterinarian's fee! The only sure prevention for this condition is to spay bitch puppies before they achieve sexual maturity. In unspayed canines, pyometritis and pyometra most commonly affect bitches that have never had a litter of puppies. However, this is not a sufficient reason for allowing unspayed bitches to have puppies.

When uterine infections affect a valuable breeding bitch, it is usually worth trying to treat the condition nonsurgically—at least for a trial period of time—in the hope of salvaging her as a breeder. If the conservative therapy fails, she can then be treated surgically in order to save her life.

Feeding

Mixed-breeds Require Nutritious Dog Food

Commercial Foods

Carefully balanced canine diets that, when fed exclusively, will completely meet or exceed the nutritional requirements for dogs are now available. Some foods are more palatable than others, and you may find that for the same amount of money, you can buy a substantially greater volume of one or two compared to others of equal nutritive value. Commercially prepared dog foods are supplied in dry, semimoist, and moist canned forms. The greatest difference between these three major divisions is their moisture content.

High quality canned foods are the most expensive when you compute their high moisture content, which often amounts to approximately 75 percent. This makes canned dog food a costly convenience.

Individual packages of burger-like semimoist dog foods are lightweight, nutritious, and readily accepted by most dogs, but they are formulated with sugar and sugarlike substances and propylene glycols in order to prevent spoilage. Although neither of these classes of ingredients is now known to be harmful, there are some nutritional experts who doubt their safety in a regular diet. Futhermore, the canned and semimoist diets are too soft to give your dog's gums and teeth needed exercise.

The remaining class of commercial diets is the dry kibble and meal type. Many are nearly as palatable as the canned and semimoist foods and have the added advantages of lightweight per volume of product, as well as firmness that provides jaw, gum, and tooth exercise. The larger sizes of kibble require active chewing that greatly aids in keeping the teeth clean and free of plaque and tartar accumulation. Some kibbled diets contain sodium levels that may be excessive for some dogs. Your veterinarian should be consulted as to what should be fed to your dog, particularly if it is older or if it has a medical history that would call for a restricted sodium intake.

An occasional treat of fat-free, boned meat, fish, or fowl is welcome, but should not be fed as a staple to your dog. Such a diet is likely to be grossly unbalanced with respect to vitamins, minerals, protein, fat, carbohydrate, and fiber content. Furthermore, dietary gastrointestinal and allergic disturbances are much less likely to occur when dogs are fed scientifically formulated commercial diets.

Several factors determine the amount of food to be fed: the stage of life; physical size of the dog; its metabolic size (which is not identical to weight); weather and/or housing arrangement in which the dog is maintained; reproductive activity; amount of exercise or work that the dog is expected to perform; and the comparative quality of the food itself.

Puppies eat much more food per unit of their body weight because they are building new tissues and using an enormous amount of energy. The gross size of a dog will naturally dictate that larger dogs should be fed a greater volume of food than smaller ones, but the metabolic rates of smaller dogs are correspondingly higher than those of the larger ones. Dogs living outdoors in cold weather expend substantial energy just keeping warm. Both reproductively active stud male dogs and brood bitches must be fed a greater amount of high-quality food than animals of the same size and age who are not being employed as breeders. A lactating bitch needs more food because of the amount of energy expended in producing milk for her puppies. Hard-working dogs or those given much exercise require more total nutrients than less active canines.

Purchasing the cheapest brand of dog food is false economy because some of these nonbrand, or "generic" animal feeds lack one or more essential nutrients. Over the intermediate to long term, such so-called "bargain" brands may result in veterinary fees that far outweigh the modest savings that were realized originally.

Table Scraps

Most table scraps may be very palatable to your dog but should not be fed as a regular ration. As a

Feeding

Some food scraps should never be fed to your dog, nor should you allow your pet to take them from the waste container.

special treat, carefully boned and fat-trimmed lean meat scraps can be mixed with your dog's regular commercial dog food. If they are fed too often, though, your dog may refuse to accept its own diet in the expectation that you will give in and feed it what you eat. High fat "goodies" left over from parties frequently are responsible for severe bouts of diarrhea and/or vomiting in pets.

Special prescription diets formulated for older dogs, or for those suffering from heart or kidney disease, intestinal disorders, food-related allergies, or other problems do lack flavor. The addition of a small amount of garlic powder or dried onion flakes can substantially improve the special diet's palatability without changing its sodium salt or protein content.

Feeding a Puppy

Puppies will begin to nibble on kibbled puppy foods even before they are weaned. By the time they are about six weeks old, most of their dietary intake should consist of commercially prepared puppy fare. Despite claims to the contrary by their manufacturers, there is little substantive difference among major brands. To date, however, one new product, Purina's O*N*E, has been developed to be fed throughout the entire lifetime of a dog, varying only the amount fed during any particular growth or maintenance life phase. Feeding instructions are published by all dog food manufacturers on the bags or boxes in which their products are shipped. These recommendations should be followed faithfully.

Cow's milk in its fresh whole or low-butterfat forms may not be tolerated by some young puppies, and older dogs. This is because many animals lack a specific enzyme, lactase, which is required to digest and assimilate milk sugar (lactose). Many of these milk-sensitive dogs will, however, tolerate cultured cow's milk products such as buttermilk, yogurt, and cottage or farmer's cheese. Many dogs accept pasteurized fresh goat's milk without experiencing digestive upsets.

Feeding a Mature Dog

Maintain the particular commercial diet on which your dog has grown to maturity, until or unless your veterinarian advises you to change to something else. Pregnancy, lactation, and strenuous work or exercise will necessitate increasing the amount of food fed whereas obesity and inactivity will necessitate reducing the amount fed.

Organ meats, especially liver, may cause diarrhea in many dogs. Although a small amount may be welcomed as a treat, it must be cooked before feeding. A good supplement to an otherwise standardized diet is beef heart that has been boiled in a small amount of water, with a few sliced onions and carrots; the resulting broth can then be mixed with your dog's kibbled ration.

Our dogs have always been fed moderate amounts of fresh, raw vegetables and fruit—apples, oranges, carrots, cabbage, broccoli, cauliflower, brussels sprouts, rutabagas, bean sprouts, and other

Feeding

produce in season. Freshly prepared unsalted popcorn and occasional almonds and peanuts are special treats. These nutritious foods are rich in vitamins, minerals, and fiber and, with the exception of the nuts, are very low in calories. A confession: the major reason for feeding such items is that our dogs have always been very fond of them!

All dogs require essential fatty acids, readily available from far safer sources than high-cholesterol waste animal fats. The notion that dogs need bacon grease or tallow to develop and maintain a sleek coat is foolishness: these saturated fats are no better for your dog than they are for you.

Feeding a Pregnant Bitch

The expanding girth of a pregnant bitch as her fetuses developed correlates to her greatly increased appetite. During the last trimester, or third, of the pregnancy, the fetuses grow enormously and their dam's food intake correspondingly increases severalfold. New tissues are being synthesized to form the organs of each puppy during this critical period. If the bitch is not fed a sufficient amount of high quality nutrients during this time, her fetuses will benefit at her expense: calcium salts will be mobilized from her skeleton; protein will be sacrificed from her muscles; fats will be drawn from her once ample stores.

Only high-quality commercial dog foods should be fed to a pregnant bitch. Other than modest supplementation with skim milk, buttermilk, or low-fat yogurt, special vitamins and minerals are not necessary. As your bitch's weight increases, she will have to be fed a correspondingly greater amount of food each day. Rather than expect her to consume all of her needed daily food intake at one time, it is best to divide her meals into two or three smaller ones. It is vital that your pregnant bitch always has a ready supply of fresh clean water available at all times. During the late stages of pregnancy, your bitch's kidneys will encounter ever-increasing demands to rid her system of her own body wastes plus those of her unborn fetuses.

Feeding a Nursing Bitch

Even after the delivery of a bitch's litter of puppies, the enormous nutritional and caloric demands during late pregnancy continue. The bitch will begin to secrete a volume of milk almost immediately, and her dietary requirements will increase vastly in order to satisfy the needs of her puppies. A small dog can easily use more than 1,500 calories daily just in secreting her nutritious high-protein milk. Add to this the amount of food needed just to maintain her body weight and health, and the total can exceed 1,850–2,000 calories required during a 24-hour period. This amount of food would be sufficient to satisfy the nutritional requirement of a young adult human. Depending upon her weight and number of puppies, a large dog would require two to three times this amount.

Skim milk or buttermilk, unflavored low milk-butterfat yogurt and cottage cheese or farmer's cheese are beneficial supplements. The fiber content in fresh fruits such as sliced unpeeled apples will help the bitch from becoming constipated. I recommend the addition of freshly grated carrots for several of my lactating bitch patients as a source of more fiber and carotene. Although it is possible to overdose with preformed vitamin A, toxicity is avoided when its precursor, beta carotene, is fed as carotene-rich foods such as leafy green, orange, and yellow vegetables.

Fresh water must be available to the nursing bitch at all times.

Feeding Newly Weaned Puppies

As early as three weeks of age, puppies will begin to nibble solid food. It can be offered in small

Feeding

amounts several times daily. The puppies will be eating more solid food and spending less time nursing by the time they are five weeks old. At about six weeks of age, they should be completely weaned, separated from their dam, and sent to new homes. To help prevent intestinal disturbances, generally it is best for new owners to continue feeding the same product that the original owners were using. If for some reason a change must be made, it must be accomplished gradually over 10 to 14 days. Diarrhea usually can be controlled by feeding frequent small meals of boiled rice or infant rice cereal mixed with cottage cheese or a small amount of boiled chicken. Small amounts of buttermilk, unflavored yogurt, and/or goat's milk also may be fed. To avoid food spoilage, offer only that amount that will be consumed within a 15-minute period.

Fresh water must be available at all times.

General Feeding Tips

Puppies should be fed five to six times a day until they are about eight to ten weeks old; three to four times a day until they are twelve to fourteen weeks old; twice daily until they are about six months old; and once daily thereafter.

We have always fed our adult dogs in the morning. By evening time, they have digested and assimilated their meal and, after their last evening walk or run, have passed their stools.

To encourage your dog to be businesslike in its eating habits, place only enough food in the dish that can be consumed during a 15-minute period.

Nondisposable food dishes must be cleaned routinely. The water bowl should be cleaned and refilled at least once daily; more often if it becomes contaminated with food particles washed from your dog's whiskers.

Devotion between children and mixed-bred dogs started long before the legendary Little Orphan Annie–Sandy friendship and continues into the present day. And then, as now, the canine functions both as inseparable friend and, when necessary, fierce protector.

Training

Housebreaking

As soon as it arrives at your home you should begin to housebreak your new puppy. Puppies, like infants, are stimulated to urinate and defecate when they are fed. Knowing this fact will make it easier to train your new dog to carry out these normal functions in an appropriate place outside the home in an area selected by you.

You should take your puppy outside immediately after feeding. At first when the puppy does as expected, it will be only a coincidence. Reach down and praise the dog, speak in an encouraging fashion and say "What a *good* doggie!" while patting it gently all the time.

If you live in an apartment or do not have a yard in which your puppy can exercise and eliminate, you should select a small room or an isolated site in one room and cover it with clean newspaper. Immediately after the puppy awakens or has eaten a meal, take it to the paper-covered area and wait until it urinates, which should not take very long. Praise each performance. If, as is quite normal during the first few days of training, your puppy has an "accident" and fails to visit its assigned toilet spot, you can place a *small* amount of its urine on a piece of absorbent cotton or bathroom tissue and deposit in onto the fresh newspaper so that a familiar scent is left. Only a few drops are necessary to accomplish this. When soiled, the newspaper must be removed and replaced with a fresh supply. As the days pass, reduce the size of the floor area covered until only a spot the size of an opened newspaper is left. You must remember that dogs are unable to read; your puppy is in the process of being trained to consider paper as a place on which to deposit its bodily wastes; if you carelessly leave an important document on the floor unattended, your puppy may see it as nothing more than a novel place to use as a toilet!

Your new puppy should be well on its way to being housebroken in about a week if your training is successful. Occasional lapses will invariably occur, but these will become uncommon events as the puppy matures and its ability to retain its urine and stools develops.

When we had just acquired a six-week-old puppy, we decided to leave the housebreaking chores to our twelve-year-old son. We contracted to pay him 10 cents per hour for his efforts. A warm sleeping bag was placed in our kitchen each evening, and our son and his new companion slept together next to a door leading onto our garden. Each time the puppy stirred in her sleep or got up, our son would arise and take it outdoors. Within a record time of only about three days, the puppy was almost completely housebroken! You might wish to try this method for your new puppy if your family and living circumstances permit it. This was the only time that I relented and recommended that our dog sleep with one of us, but in my opinion, the circumstances—and results—merited that permissiveness!

Adjusting to Collar and Leash

On the very first day that you bring it into your home, a soft training collar should be placed around your new puppy's neck. The newer varieties of pliant woven nylon collars, which are both lightweight and washable, are ideally suited for young puppies. Frequently the puppy will not even notice that it is wearing it.

The Halti head collar is a newly patented training device that is designed to fit over the animal's muzzle and the back of its neck in such a manner that it does not encircle the entire neck. When

Although the results of mixed breeding may sometimes be amusing, they are also often strikingly handsome. In many cases, the contribution of a particular breed can be clearly discerned. Note, for example, the obvious Siberian chatracteristics of the dog shown below left.

applied correctly, the head collar humanely turns the head in the direction that you desire without choking the dog. In practice, this device is readily accepted with little, if any, resistance.

A leash, however, is usually accepted—until it is used to turn the puppy in the direction in which *you* wish to walk. Typically, a naive puppy will pull in every direction. Even especially stubborn puppies will learn to be led while tethered to you by a leash if given encouragement and positive reinforcement. All dogs should be leash trained so that the owner can exert some control over their pet during even the rare instances when a leash is required, e.g. when you must take your pet to the veterinarian.

It is imperative that you never use the leash as a punitive object. Your puppy should not associate a leash with unpleasantness.

Correcting Bad Habits

On occasion, even the very best mannered dog will behave in a fashion that is contrary to your wishes. Remember that dogs are intelligent creatures and most crossbreds are especially bright and responsive to their human companions.

It is important that you correct a negative behavioral trait in a manner that will convey to your pet that you will not tolerate what it is doing. You must be consistent in correction, and each time you apply corrective action it must be aimed at instruction rather than punishment. Even a very young dog, if socialized properly, will strive to please its owner.

Jumping on People

Few things are more frightening to young children, or more annoying to adults, than to have a dog jump up on them. A set of muddy pawprints rarely is welcomed by anyone wearing clean clothes, and a dog's claws can cause deep scratches in tender skin.

A firm command, "down!" delivered together

One means for discouraging your dog from jumping on people.

with an immediate movement of one of your knees so that it strikes the offending dog squarely on its upended chest need only be done a few times to convey the correction. Alternatively, a Halti head collar can be used with excellent results because the leash attaches to a metal ring fitted beneath the dog's chin. The dog cannot jump if its head, now controlled with a collar and leash, is restricted to a horizontal plane.

If your dog merely places its forepaws on you as it stands, say "down!" as you gently place the pressure of your foot on the dog's rear toes.

By using any or a combination of these techniques, your dog will soon learn that what it has been doing will not be tolerated by you or other humans.

Inappropriate Barking

Barking at strange sounds or people is entirely normal, and positive, for your dog. Incessant howling or baying, though, particularly at night, is justifiable cause for complaints from your neighbors.

You must immediately command, "no!" when this behavior occurs, and comfort your dog so that it can see that there is no threat to you from outside. If necessary, command the dog to lie down near you, and each time it begins to vocalize, repeat the correction.

If your neighbors complain that your dog barks in your absence, you will have to take severe action to stop this disturbance once and for all. There are electronic devices built in to dog collars which, when activated by the sound of the dog's own bark, will deliver a mild shock to the skin immediately beneath the collar's electrodes. In some instances, these collars can be rented for a specified time from your veterinarian or local pet shop.

A procedure to debark a dog is technically termed *ventriculochordectomy*, and is no more serious than a properly performed tonsillectomy. Most veterinarians will release the dog on the same day of surgery. The necessary surgical anesthetic is one whose effects are short-lived, and the total fee is relatively modest. The procedure will render a dog's barking efforts no louder than a harsh cough that can be heard within the walls of your home but is barely perceptible through a closed front door.

This solution should be reserved for only those situations where the only other alternative is to dispose of the offending dog.

Begging for Food

You and your guests should not be annoyed by begging, when eating in your dog's presence.

The appropriate correction for this behavior is a firm "no!" or "down!" delivered with conviction. If begging was wrong yesterday, it will not be tolerated today or tomorrow, and you must not give in to those imploring brown eyes staring up from beneath your chair or table. Remember that you must be consistent. It is equally important that other household members or guests not feed your dog. If they do, your own best efforts will be in vain.

Biting and Other Overaggressive Behavior

Some members of a litter will display dominance over their more submissive siblings, even when they are very young puppies. Once they have been weaned and placed into new homes, however, they should be submissive to their human companions, not *vice versa*. If your puppy exhibits a tendency to bite or in some other way acts in an aggressive manner to humans, you must correct it immediately and with resolute firmness.

Deliver a loud and meaningful command of "no!" together with a single sharp hand slap to the flat area of the dog's ribs and shoulder. Only the palm of your hand should be used. All you wish to accomplish by this maneuver is to reinforce the message of your displeasure by a mild stinging slap. Actually, the suddenness and sound of the slap are its most effective components, and you need not be concerned that your dog will associate your hands with a threat when you employ this correction.

Never strike your dog on the top of its head or near its eyes or ears, nor under any circumstances ever employ a stick or other hard object to discipline an animal. When an infraction warrants a more severe correction, some dog trainers do recommend striking the top of the nose with an accompanying loud verbal command of "no!" or "out!" Some trainers recommend the use of a rolled newpaper with which to reinforce a correction; others eschew all corporal punishment. Although a newspaper is available in most homes and will not cause physical trauma, I believe that it is used too often and may even create situations when the dog becomes overly

Training

fearful of it—and its master.

Consistency is vitally important whenever you are training your dog. Your loud and firm verbal commands often will be all that is needed to correct aggressive misbehavior.

Inappropriate Chewing

Exploring its immediate environment by whatever means it has at its disposal is entirely normal behavior for a puppy. Dogs will employ their acute senses of smell and taste to evaluate things that are novel to their limited experience. No matter how normal, this exploration can be a source of danger to the animal and annoyance to you, its owner.

To control chewing, simply keep valuable items away from your puppy. Pick up belongings that might be chewed if left within its reach. Try to redirect the puppy's inclination to chew by providing a few things that were meant to be gnawed such as rawhide chew bones that will last for a variable time. If portions of them are chewed and are swallowed, they will be digested as food. Tough Nylabone chew bones are available from pet suppliers and are nearly indestructible, of course they are not digestible if swallowed.

Inappropriate Sexual Activity

It is only natural for a sexually mature dog to react to sexually arousing stimulation. The sexually motivated instincts of male dogs originate in a particularly ancient portion of the brain and are less readily modified by learned behavior corrections. Behavior such as mounting and attempting to mate with stuffed toys, pillows, or a person's lower leg may be triggered by any number of different stimuli. One frequent cause is the scent of a bitch in estrus. In some highly sensitive male dogs, this behavior can be induced when the dog perceives the scent of a menstruating woman.

A short term solution to this problem is a loud and firm command of "no!" accompanied by banishment to the yard or another room. For the longer

term, surgical neutering might be appropriate. Unless you have some compelling reasons for breeding your male dog, there are many sound reasons why you should consider—and act—on the long-term solution. (This is discussed in greater detail in the section on spaying and neutering. See pages 62-65.)

Chasing Cars and Bicycles

The habit of chasing cars and bicycles is a substantial danger to the dog, as well as a hazard to the humans riding. Responsible dog owners will do everything possible to prevent and stop their dogs from engaging in this behavior.

In some states a dog owner is held financially responsible for losses caused by their animal's uncontrolled behavior.

If your dog has developed the habit of chasing vehicles and you cannot or will not confine your dog to a fenced yard, you will have to use other means of restraint. One arrangement that allows freedom within a limited perimeter is a long leash attached to a large metal ring fastened to a taughtly stretched horizontal wire or clothesline. Another method employs tying the dog to a long stout nylon line, attached to the dog's choke chain training collar. The line is left very loosely coiled. When the dog starts to chase a vehicle it will suddenly and without warning reach the end of its tether and be jerked back violently. The stretchy nylon cord will prevent the sudden jolt from causing physical injury to the dog, and it will prevent the dog from achieving its goal of approaching the car or bicycle. The Halti head collar is useful for training a dog not to lunge at or chase people or their vehicles, but it is best employed when attached to a flexible leash held by its owner/trainer.

Some dog trainers have advised having an accomplice armed with a toy squirt gun loaded with dilute lemon juice or mild aqueous ammonia solution purposely ride by on a bicycle several times until the dog runs out and starts to chase; at this point, the cyclist squirts the dog in the face. Although in legal terms this might be interpreted as entrapment, it is very effective: after one or two experiences of having a disagreeable yet harmless substance sprayed in the face, most dogs will soon associate the act of chasing with the distasteful correction.

If You Encounter More Severe Disciplinary Problems

Disciplinary or behavioral problems usually can be resolved by simple home obedience training. Some people, however, are just not capable of showing authority—even to a dog; others, for one reason or another, cannot discipline a dog. In these instances, is is best to seek the counsel of a professional dog trainer.

If deep-seated psychological abnormalities are found in your dog, you may wish to "cut your losses" as soon as possible. Mental illness is known to affect animals, but the psychoanalytic methods of human therapy are not appropriate to dogs.

Teaching Some Practical Tricks

Sit!

While attached to its leash, place the puppy, on your left side. As you give the command "sit!" place your hand firmly behind the knee area of its rear legs, pushing downward. Repeat this maneuver, each time commanding the dog to "sit!" until your puppy will obey your command without having to be pushed down on its hocks. Each time the puppy obeys, tell it what a splendid creature it is.

Stay!

To "stay" in place—even when you walk away—is one of the most useful commands that you

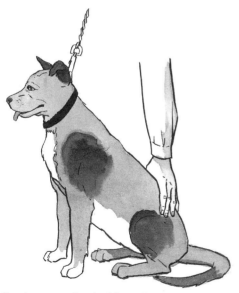

Give the command to *sit* while gently pushing your dog's hindquarters into a sitting position and keeping its head had elevated with the leash.

Stay. Use the flat of your hand as a visual signal while speaking the command. Be patient. This can be a very difficult lesson for your dog.

can teach your dog. Place your hand palm toward and close to the dog's face and command "stay!" in a firm voice. Start to move away after a few moments, and if the puppy begins to follow you, stop immediately and repeat the command and the hand signal.

Down!

Your dog should be trained to lie down immediately with its front legs extended in front of it. It can, if you desire, be a natural progression from the command to "sit!" or can be used independently. Give the authoritative command "stay!" as you place your hand on your dog's shoulders and apply gentle, yet firm, pressure downward. You then should stand in front of the dog and praise it for a job well done. Allow the dog to get up after a short while, and repeat the command and hand pressure until the dog obeys without hesitation.

Heel!

The well-mannered dog should walk, whether leashed or free, alongside your left leg. This is a standardized position and was developed to prevent your dog from tripping you by crossing your path. As you walk, use the leash to direct and keep the dog next to your left leg. While walking, turn to your left in a circle. Because the dog now finds itself inside of the circle, it will find that maintaining its position on your left is the easiest. When you stop walking forward, command the dog to "sit!" Again, this is the conventional way a well trained dog should behave. The Halti head collar is particularly useful for training your dog to perform this command.

Come

It is imperative that you teach this very important command using only positive reinforcement, because if your dog becomes fearful, it may hesitate to come at a vital moment. The command is taught by starting with your dog in the "sit" or "down" position. After the dog is settled in one of these

While heeling, whether leashed or free, your dog should walk alongside your left leg.

positions, command it to "stay!" Take a few steps away, turn to face your dog, and drop to a kneeling or squatting position. Beckoning with your hands, say "come!" in a soft, encouraging voice. If the dog leaves its sitting or reclining position and obeys your "come!" command, praise it lavishly. Be absolutely certain, while you are teaching your dog this command, not to act in a negative fashion.

Roll Over!

After it has learned this command, your dog will assume a position that will allow you to inspect its belly for ticks, fleas, or foreign bodies attached to the skin or fur.

While your dog is already lying down, command it to "roll over!" as you gently grasp its front legs and turn him or her onto its back and then over to the other side. Repeat the command several times; as you do it, roll your pet over onto its back. Praise each practice attempt, particularly when your dog rolls over without your using its legs as a prompt.

Training

Fetch an Object

Retrieving an object at your command is one of the easiest tricks to teach. Most dogs will chase a moving object because it is their nature to pursue moving prey. A crossbred dog with a retriever for one of its parents will possess a greater natural interest in this kind of behavior, but essentially any dog can be taught to retrieve an object.

Start with a rubber ball that is small enough to be carried easily in your dog's mouth, but sufficiently large to prevent its being swallowed.

Command your dog to "sit!" and praise it. Allow your pet to smell the ball. While your dog's attention is focused on the ball, throw it gently as you give the command "fetch!"

If your dog immediately chases the ball and returns it to you, be lavish in your praise. If the dog ignores the ball entirely or merely dawdles, pick up the ball and repeat the exercise. You may allow the dog to taste the ball by placing it in its mouth.

Once you have taught your dog to run after and pick up the ball, command it to "come!" back to you and to "sit!" in front of you. As soon as it has assumed the sitting position, gently remove the ball from its jaws and praise it heartily. Repeat the entire sequence as many times as necessary. Dogs usually will learn this trick within a day or two.

After it has mastered "fetch!" with the ball, you can substitute a rolled or folded newspaper. Soon you will be able to command your dog to fetch your paper from where the delivery person deposited it.

Carry an Object

"Fetch!" and "carry!" both center around your dog's transporting an object to you by mouth. Some retriever ancestry in a crossbred dog will facilitate its performance and training for this extremely useful command.

Place a rolled newspaper or nonresinous wooden stick between your dog's jaws. Give the command "carry!" as you do this; if your dog keeps the object in its mouth, praise it. If your dog imme-

diately drops the object, repeat the command and replace the stick or paper in its mouth. It should not take long to learn this useful trick.

Avoid an Object

Dangerous objects, strange food items, food offered by strangers, and other animals' stools are but a few of the things that many dogs will pick up. Teaching your dog to refrain from touching an object within grasping range is a very useful, even lifesaving, command.

Begin your training session with your dog on its leash and allow it to approach a tempting food item placed on the floor. As the dog bends its head down to smell and grasp the food, immediately and forcefully give the command "no!" as you give a sharp jerk on the leash. By this time, your dog should already understand "no!"

Enlist several of your friends to offer food to your dog, and each time repeat the command "no!" The firm jerk on the leash should soon be an unnecessary reinforcement to the vocal command.

Never allow anyone who does not regularly feed your dog to offer it food. Should you need to have your dog kenneled or cared for by another person in your absence, you will have to condition your pet to accept food from those strangers by having them feed it for a day or two in your presence and with your vocal praise.

Staying at Home Alone

The term "separation anxiety" has been applied to the behavior of humans and animals, when they believe they have been abandoned by their loved ones. Children left at summer camp for the first time experience separation anxiety. It is only natural for a young dog to experience this uncertainty of not knowing why it was left alone and when its owner will return.

Once your puppy has become accustomed to the

Training

concept that your home is its home also, begin training it to stay home alone without misbehaving.

Place your puppy in a small room with one or more of its favorite toys. Calmly close the door to the room, speaking to the puppy as you depart. It will probably try to squeeze out through the doorway, and you must gently, yet firmly, push it back into the room and close the door carefully. Remain relaxed and say "goodbye" as if it were the most natural thing to be leave the puppy alone.

If your puppy barks or whines, use a firm voice command of "no!" each time it vocalizes.

If your puppy remains quiet for a few minutes, open the door and praise your pet lavishly, conveying to it how happy you are to see it again, but do not overdramatize your return.

Leave your puppy alone for varying periods of time—from several minutes to several hours. Each time you return to release it from confinement, go through the ritual of praise. Try to make these periods as irregular as possible, so that your puppy cannot associate them with your daily schedule. The most important things for your puppy to learn are that you *will* return and that being alone is not a form of punishment.

Dogs who suffer from separation anxiety may chew on furniture, urinate and/or defecate while confined to a room. With thoughtful and consistent training, each of these offenses can be stopped. It is better to teach good habits from the start rather than to retrain an already misbehaving puppy.

Training for Guard Duties

You probably will not have to actually teach your young dog to be protective. If you wish to have it specifically trained for security work, it is imperative that it first be well trained in simple obedience. It is natural for a dog to protect its home territory from strangers.

When your dog hears your doorbell, it should immediately bark or growl. You should praise your dog for this quick reaction. If the dog is not already at the door, command it to "come!" and "sit!" Having a family member or friend ring the bell for you while you are in the house with your dog will help you with this training. At no time should you permit your dog to make actual contact with the "stranger." A sharp bark or two is all that you are aiming for at this point.

If you wish to have your dog trained to do more than alert you to the presence of strangers, you should consult one or more professional dog trainers for an evaluation of your dog's suitability for more aggressive guard duty.

The Responsible Dog Owner

It is no longer socially responsible for a dog owner to allow a pet companion to run free. Fewer people live on farms, ranches, and even in single family housing. A social contract must exist so that the dog will not become a nuisance to neighbors.

As citizens of an expanded community, we must assure those with whom we live that they will not be victimized by odor and noise pollution from the presence of our canine companions. A dog must never constitute a physical threat to children and other pets.

In summary, a dog should be an enriching bonus to our life; it must never become a creature that only complicates our daily existence.

In Sickness and in Health

Disease Prevention Measures

Most communicable diseases of dogs can be prevented by timely vaccination. Once devastating internal parasitic diseases are now readily controlled by appropriate medication. External parasites such as fleas, ticks, mites, and lice are now easily killed and their reinfestation repelled.

Vaccinations

It is always a sad task for me as a veterinarian to inform a dog owner that a puppy has a serious disease that could have been prevented so easily with proper immunization. Because antibodies that your puppy acquired from its previously immunized bitch slowly diminish, at about eight weeks of age the puppy may have lost its resistance to common canine infectious diseases.

The common diseases against which young puppies are routinely immunized are canine distemper, infectious canine hepatitis, canine parvoviral gastroenteritis, canine coronaviral gastroenteritis, parainfluenza, leptospirosis, and rabies. Polyvalent vaccines that contain the immunizing agents for the first six diseases are available, so your dog will have to receive only one broad-scope injection plus another for rabies vaccination. This immunization is repeated at eight, twelve, and sixteen weeks of age. Rabies immunization is given at four months of age.

A yearly visit to your family veterinarian offers your dog an opportunity for a thorough physical examination and routine prophylactic immunization, and a chance for you to ask any questions regarding your pet's health and care. These annual physical examinations and booster vaccinations usually are modestly priced and represent valuable "insurance" that your dog will live a longer and more healthful life. Some conditions such as tumors, diabetes, heart disease, and eye and dental disorders may be detected while they may easily be remedied but, if diagnosed after they have existed for a prolonged time, may prove to be far more serious. A yearly physical examination is particularly valuable for unspayed bitches and intact male dogs, especially after they reach middle age. If a restricted or special diet is necessary, your veterinarian can provide information on its use.

Canine Distemper: The virus of canine distemper is spread from dog to dog via eating, drinking, or inhaling infective materials in mucous secretions, vomitus, or stools. The virus may be spread by humans that have handled sick dogs shedding the virus. Infective virus also may be carried on the shoes of people who have walked where an infected dog has discharged the contents of its stomach, intestines, or mucus from its lungs.

Canine distemper is characterized by a large number of signs or symptoms. Early in the disease, the infected dog will exhibit a fever of from 103.5 to 105.5 degrees Fahrenheit, but the dog's body temperature soon decreases to the normal 100.5 to 102.5F. only to become elevated again in about two days. Typical signs are exhaustion, vomiting, diarrhea, tonsillitis, coughing, mucus-laden discharges from the nose and eyes, hardening of the foot, toe, and nose pads, and central nervous system (brain and spinal cord) disorders ranging from minor nervous tics to major convulsions. Classically, if any four of these signs are seen together, a tentative diagnosis of canine distemper should be considered. Often the affected dog appears to recover from the first signs of gastrointestinal and respiratory disease, only to begin to exhibit signs of severe brain damage about six weeks after the illness first began. The death rate from distemper may be as high as 75 percent.

All dogs should receive yearly booster immunizations for canine distemper as part of their annual physical examination and necessary prophylactic vaccinations.

Infectious Canine Hepatitis: The virus of infectious canine hepatitis is not infectious for humans and is unrelated to infectious hepatitis in people. It is most commonly a clinical disease of the young, nonimmunized dog, particularly one whose bitch was unvaccinated, rather than the older dog where it usually is asymptomatic or at most a mild disease. Also, it is responsible for the abortion, stillbirth, and/or birth of weak puppies.

The physical signs of infectious canine hepatitis are fatigue, tonsillitis, loss of appetite, fever, vomiting, diarrhea, and abdominal pain. If there is substantial liver damage, the whites of the dog's eyes often may change to bright yellow. If the dog survives for several weeks, its corneas may become cloudy and milky blue-white; this alteration lasts for a week or so and then slowly returns to normal.

The infectious hepatitis virus is shed in the urine and feces of infected dogs. The death loss rate may exceed 60 percent in unprotected puppies.

It is accepted practice to include infectious canine hepatitis vaccine in your dog's annual booster immunizations.

Canine Parvoviral Gastroenteritis: Canine parvoviral gastroenteritis is spread from an infected dog to a susceptible (nonimmunized) dog by contact with feces, vomitus, or blood. The virus also can be carried on the shoes and clothing of humans exposed to infective material.

In young and adult dogs, parvovirus infection manifests itself in acute fatigue, high fever, profuse vomiting, and diarrhea (often bloody), and profound dehydration from the loss of body fluids. In unborn fetuses, the heart muscle often is damaged severely; many puppies born after having contracted parvovirus while in the uterus of the bitch subsequently die of heart failure.

Relatively new to North American dogs, canine parvovirus made its debut as a severe epidemic disease in the late 1970s. The virus that is responsible for this disease is similar to, but not identical to, the agent that is responsible for causing feline distemper (panleukopenia).

Yearly booster vaccinations are recommended; they are usually included in polyvalent vaccines for the major diseases of dogs.

Canine Coronaviral Gastroenteritis: Superficially very similar in signs and symptoms to canine parvoviral gastroenteritis, this disease of young puppies usually is substantially milder and less deadly. Some dogs may become severely ill and may even die from this condition, but these are unusual cases. One consistent feature of this disease that helps differentiate it from parvovirus infection is the yellow-orange, occasionally bloody diarrhea.

The major signs of coronavirus infection in puppies and young dogs are a sudden onset of vomiting and diarrhea, loss of appetite, dehydration, and a mild fever. The duration of the disease is seven to ten days.

Vaccination against coronavirus is somewhat controversial and the vaccines may be of questionable efficacy.

Parainfluenza: Parainfluenza virus is spread from one dog to others by contact of unvaccinated dogs with the coughed-up mucus and other wastes from carrier canines. Humans also can carry the virus on their clothing and shoes. Another disease agent, the bacterium, *Bortadella bronchosepticum* has been implicated in causing a kennel cough-like disease.

Commonly called "kennel cough" because it causes persistent coughing, infection with canine parainfluenza virus or a combination of parainfluenza and other viruses or bacteria produce upper and lower respiratory illnesses. Although usually not life threatening, these disorders are unpleasant for the affected dogs and, because of the almost constant and often protracted coughing, are very annoying for the dogs' owners—and neighbors. The coughing usually can be controlled with anti-cough medications prescribed by your veterinarian.

Prophylactic immunization with parainfluenza virus vaccine has been shown to be effective in protecting dogs from "kennel cough." A booster vaccination should be given yearly as part of a routine immunization program.

Leptospirosis: Whereas the other prevalent infectious diseases of dogs are viral, leptospirosis is a bacterial infection common to many species of mammals, including humans. The leptospiral bacteria are shed in the urine of carrier animals, and infection occurs when susceptible dogs are exposed to that urine. Even dogs that have recovered several months earlier from active leptospirosis can continue to act as carriers of the disease to unvaccinated dogs. It is possible for humans to be infected through contact with an infected dog's urine. Strict hygiene is essential when dealing with a proven case of leptospirosis; this includes careful washing of hands, the use of disposable food and water bowls, and household bleach disinfection of all surfaces that were in contact with urine, vomitus, or stools.

The signs of the acute phase of leptospirosis may mimic those of both canine distemper and infectious canine hepatitis: fatigue, loss of appetite, fever, tonsillitis, ocular or nasal discharge, vomiting, abdominal pain, and muscular pain. The white portion of the eyes may become yellow, as they do with infectious canine hepatitis and, in severe cases, the skin and gums may become yellowish.

Most dogs infected with the leptospirosis bacteria will recover with appropriate and aggressive antibiotic and supportive therapy, but a prolonged period of convalescence may be required before they return to full health. Dogs should receive annual booster immunization for leptospirosis.

Rabies: Known from earliest historic times as a menace to humans, rabies remains a justifiably much-feared disease of warm-blooded animals. Many species of wildlife, such as bats, skunks,

Table I
Quick Reference Chart For Canine Infectious Diseases

Sign or Symptom	Canine Distemper	Infectious Canine Heptitis	Parvoviral Gastroenteritis	Coronaviral Gastroenteritis	Parainfluenza	Leptospirosis	Rabies
Vomiting	X	X	X	X		X	
Diarrhea	X	X	X*	X**		X	
"Cold" or "Flu"	X	†		X	X	†	
Convulsions, Seizures, "Fits"	X	†				†	X
Hardening of the Foot and Nose Pads	X						

*The diarrhea seen in cases of parvoviral gastroenteritis often is light-gray, yellow-gray, or hemorrhagic
**The diarrhea seen in coronaviral gastroenteritis often is yellow-orange, occasionally bloody.
†A variable sign in this disease.

foxes, raccoons, and feral (wild) cats and dogs serve as natural reservoirs of the virus.

Rabies in dogs may take either of two forms: in the "furious" form, the dog is extremely aggressive and often attacks other animals, humans, or even inanimate objects; in the "dumb" form, the dog becomes extremely lethargic and gradually lapses into stupor. In either case, there is a great tendency for the infected victim to avoid water; hence the common term for the disease, "hydrophobia." One can become infected when the saliva from either form of a rabid animal enters an open skin wound.

Rabies is deadly. Therefore, your dog must be vaccinated at four to six months of age and every two to three years thereafter (depending upon the state in which you reside and the type of vaccine used). Very effective vaccines have made the occurrence of rabies in properly vaccinated dogs extremely rare.

Worming

Roundworms of several species, tapeworms, hookworms, whipworms, *and* some protozoa are the major gastrointestinal parasites of dogs.

Roundworms: Because some forms of worms exist in tissues other than those of the gastrointestinal tract of the pregnant bitch and are unaffected by routine deworming treatments, even the very best kennels encounter the problem of roundworm infestation in puppies that are born from previously dewormed bitches. It is important therefore that all new puppies have their stools examined microscopically for the presence of roundworm eggs. By the time the puppy is ten weeks old this examination should be repeated at least once more because it may take that long for the immature worms that were transferred to the puppy across the placenta and from mammary glands from the bitch to migrate through the puppy's liver and lungs and eventually reach its intestines. Once present in the stomach and intestines, roundworms may make their presence ·nown by being vomited by the puppy, but if your puppy does not vomit them, you may never know that they are infesting your pet. Ideally, the stools should be rechecked when the puppy reaches fourteen weeks of age. Each time the stools are found to be positive for worm eggs the puppy should be properly dewormed with one or more medications called anthelminthics.

If your puppy is shown to be free of roundworms on two successive stool examinations, it will not have to be dewormed further unless it becomes reinfested by ingesting worm eggs from an infected environment.

Tapeworms: Ribbonlike tapeworm segments called *proglottids* are sometimes seen either on the surfaces of your dog's formed stools or crawling from its anus. Soon after they are exposed to air, these segments become desiccated, shrink, and look like grains of rice.

The most common species of tapeworms affecting urban dogs is *Dipylidium caninum*, which requires a common dog flea as its intermediate host. The larval fleas ingest eggs that are enclosed within the proglottids, and intermediate stages of the tapeworms soon develop within the fleas' bodies. Soon after being ingested by a dog as it grooms itself, the infected fleas release the immature tapeworms into the digestive canal of the dog; there the immature tapeworms become adults and complete their life cycle by producing more eggs.

Your dog may be infested by other species of tapeworms. Some utilize small rodents and rabbits as intermediate hosts, and one tapeworm species, called *Echinococcus granulosus*, infests dogs by using sheep, goats, deer, and even bears as hosts. This species of tapeworm poses a public health hazard to humans also because people can contract the worm by accidentally ingesting their eggs which may be on the fur of infected dogs.

Because of their life cycles and physiological characteristics, tapeworms are not effectively treated by over-the-counter medications for roundworms. Several excellent antitapeworm medications are available from your family veterinarian.

In Sickness and in Health

The life cycle of the common dog flea and one of the kinds of tapeworms.

To keep your dog free from tapeworms, it is essential that it also be kept free from fleas.

Hookworms: Like roundworms, hookworms can be transmitted from an infected mother dog to her unborn puppies. The tiny immature worms travel across the placental membranes from which the fetal puppies are nourished. Unlike roundworms, hookworms can kill young dogs rapidly. Infestation often results in severe anemia within only a few weeks after birth. Older dogs also can become infested when they ingest infected material deposited by another animal, or by walking upon moist soil contaminated by infective immature hookworm larvae.

Hookworm infestation is diagnosed by microscopic examination of your puppy's stools.

If your puppy is shown to be infested, it must be effectively treated by an appropriate medication dispensed by your veterinarian. You and other members of your household should wash hands carefully after handling your dog and properly dispose of its stools so that further transmission of infective larvae is prevented.

Whipworms: whipworms also can be a problem with pet dogs, although they are not encountered as commonly as the other forms of worms mentioned. These parasites usually take up residence in your dog's cecum, the blind pouchlike counterpart of the human vermiform appendix; here they often cause considerable inflammation and discomfort. An infested dog often bites and chews at its flank in attempts to ease its pain.

Whipworm infestation diagnosis is made by finding their characteristic eggs in the stools of infected dogs.

Whipworms can be difficult to treat because of their preference for the cecum. Today several new drugs have proved effective.

Heartworms: The heartworm, *Dirofilaria immitis*, is a significant parasite of dogs in many areas of North America. The life cycle of the heartworm requires one of several species of mosquito. Adult heartworms reside in the chambers of the heart and pulmonary vessels where they mate. The young worms, called *microfilaria*, are released into the bloodstream, where they are ingested with the blood meals that female mosquitoes must have before they can produce fertile eggs. The microfilaria are then deposited onto the skin surface of dogs where they migrate through the skin puncture made by the infected mosquitoes.

It is possible to rid an infested dog of its adult heartworms, although treatment entails the use of some toxic drugs that must be administered only under controlled conditions by a veterinarian experienced in this therapy.

Veterinarians, rather than placing the major emphasis on treatment, now recommend prevention of infection with microfilaria by giving dogs who live in or travel through heartworm-endemic areas an effective medication called diethylcarbamazine, sold under a variety of trade names. The drug is given daily, usually as a palatable tablet that most dogs will accept as a treat. It must be given only to dogs that have been shown on laboratory examination of their blood to be *free* from microfilariae and, thus free from infestation with adult heartworms. If your dog is already infested, it must NOT be treated with diethylcarbamazine.

Recently another antiheartworm medication, ivermectin (Heartgard[30]-Merck-Agvet), has come onto the market. It has the advantage of being effective when given only once every 30 days. It is formulated in three dosage levels to match the size of the animal.

The yearly cost for protecting a large dog is approximately $35 to $50; for a small dog, the cost is approximately $18 to $24, depending upon the weight of each dog and the brand of product used.

Flea and Tick Control

Crossbred canines, like pedigreed purebreed dogs, can serve as unwilling hosts to fleas and ticks. Not being very discriminating in their choice of victims, unpleasant parasites also can bite humans.

A wide variety of excellent flea and tick sprays and powders fortunately are available from veterinarians and some pet suppliers. Many of these products not only kill the fleas and ticks, but also repel reinfestation. If you experience a flea or tick problem, one or more of these products should be used routinely and according to the package instructions. Where appropriate, you should spray your premises to eradicate breeding populations of these parasites in your household and yard.

Specific skin conditions related to flea infestation are discussed in the section Disorders of the Coat and Skin (See pages 73-74).

Procedures You Should Master

Obtaining Your Dog's Temperature

A stubby rectal thermometer, available from any drugstore, should be used to obtain your dog's rectal temperature. The technique is simple; if done with gentleness, it will not be particularly unpleasant to your pet.

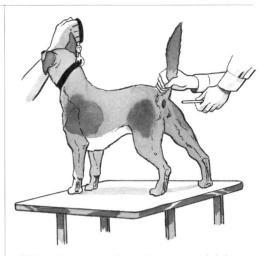

While taking your dog's rectal temperature, it is important not to allow it to sit on the thermometer.

Be certain to drive the mercury down into the bulb-reservoir of the thermometer before using it, by shaking it downward with a snapping action. The level of the mercury should be below the 96-degree Fahrenheit mark on the glass barrel.

With a small amount of petroleum jelly or similar product, lubricate the tip of the thermometer. The instrument must be inserted at least two inches and left in place for at least two minutes. During the time that the thermometer is inserted within your dog's rectum, DO NOT ALLOW THE DOG TO SIT DOWN. Have a helper hold the dog's head erect with the aid of its collar and leash or support your pet's rear quarters with one hand placed beneath and between its rear legs. Praise your dog for its good behavior.

After you have obtained your dog's temperature, wipe the thermometer with an alcohol-moistened tissue, shake the mercury down into the bulb, and replace the delicate instrument back into its storage case.

The normal temperature range of dogs is 100.5 to 102.5 degrees F. Generally small dogs possess baseline body temperatures slightly higher than larger dogs. This is a reflection of the higher metabolic rate in smaller animals, as compared with larger creatures.

Giving Medications

Tablets and Capsules: While you speak gently and confidently to your dog, hold its muzzle with your nondominant hand and elevate its head to about a 45-degree angle. With your dominant hand, use your finger to open the jaw by pushing down on the central teeth. Place the tablet or capsule over the back of the tongue, as far as you can. Remove your fingers, close the dog's mouth, and stroke its neck or rub its nose vigorously.

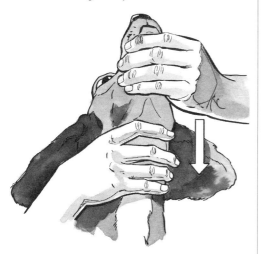

To encourage your dog to swallow its medication, you can either rub its nose or massage its throat while elevating its head.

In some instances, some pills and capsules can be hidden in a small amount of the dog's favorite food. Alternatively, the contents of some capsules may be mixed with food; this technique is not appropriate with medications that have a bad taste. Giving the medication directly is usually most effective.

Liquid Medications: Tip your dog's head back slightly with your nondominant hand. With the third finger of your dominant hand, open the jaw by pushing down on the lower central teeth. Using a plastic (<u>not glass</u>) eyedropper or metal spoon, place the required amount of liquid medication over the back of the tongue or into the dog's cheek. Close its mouth, and rub your pet's nose pad vigorously; this last maneuver will induce the dog to swallow and lick its nose. Before you release your dog, praise it lavishly for its fine cooperation.

Obtaining Your Dog's Pulse

The most convenient place to find the pulse beat of your dog is on the inner side of either hind leg, a few inches above the knee joint. As you feel the inside of the leg at this point, you will find a shallow groove in which the large femoral artery and vein lie. With gentle pressure from your fingertip you will feel the arterial pulse that corresponds to each contraction of your dog's left ventricle. Using a watch, time the number of pulse beats for 15 or 30 seconds and multiply the number of beats by either four or two, as appropriate, to know the pulse rate per minute.

Restraining Your Dog

You should always restrain your dog with a proper leash attached to its collar when walking it on crowded city streets or when taking it to the veterinarian. Having your companion properly leashed will prevent tragic accidents when you encounter other dogs on the street. At the veterinary clinic or hospital, other pet owners may be in the reception area; having each animal controlled on a leash or confined to a carrier will be appreciated and will make everyone's visit safe and more enjoyable.

If your dog is an intact bitch and if she is in heat, it is only courteous and proper that you do not walk

In Sickness and in Health

her in the neighborhood until her estrus period is completed.

To Spay or Neuter or Not to Spay or Neuter, *That* is the Question

Whereas it is exciting and educational to have your female dog experience parenthood, it nevertheless requires an enormous amount of effort to care for a pregnant and nursing bitch properly and to maintain an actively breeding stud dog adequately. There is no shortage of adoptable dogs; unless yours is such an exceptionally fine animal (of either sex), you should consider having it spayed or neutered.

Advantages of Spaying

The foremost advantage to spaying a bitch puppy is that it will render her permanently sterile. Estrous cycling, which is often inconvenient, will not occur after the removal of your bitch's ovaries and uterus. If a bitch is spayed before her first estrus, it is very unlikely that she will develop malignant breast tumors; any mammary tumors that do occur will almost always be benign. The possibility of any ovarian and uterine problems will be eliminated and most vaginal disorders will be avoided.

If the spay operation is performed before the bitch's onset of sexual maturity, the bitch will be far less likely to become obese—unless you or other family members grossly overfeed her. A bitch puppy that is spayed early usually will retain her playfulness well into her later years. Data now suggests that the spayed bitch lives a longer and healthier life, particularly after her tenth year of age.

Disadvantages of Spaying

The *only* disadvantage to spaying a bitch is the loss of her fertility. The popular belief that spaying transforms a bitch into a fat, lazy, lackluster and personality-flawed creature is not true. As has been observed by ALPO Pet Center, "There are no fat dogs...just overfed dogs!" Proper diet and exercise will keep any dog in good trim.

Advantages of Neutering a Male Dog

If a male dog is neutered when it is between ten to twelve months of age, it already will have learned to "hike" its leg when it urinates and most likely will not have acquired most of the mature sexual behavioral characteristics that develop during its second year of life. If neutered early in life, a male dog is much less likely to become obese or lose any of its positive personality traits.

Many of the disorders of the aging intact male, such as testicular and scrotal tumors, perineal hernias, and perianal gland tumors are closely related to the influence of male sex hormones so the neutered male dog usually will be spared.

The greatest benefit of neutering a male dog from the immediate practical standpoint is that once the source of male hormones is removed, the socially unacceptable sexual behavior that many house or apartment-raised intact dogs display is *prevented*. This is particularly true in the case of males that are sexually naive at the time that they are neutered.

Male dogs that have been neutered early in their young adult life generally retain their splendid personalities and do not grow obese. The neutered dog tends to display somewhat less aggressiveness towards other dogs and is much less likely to engage in dogfights. Research has shown that neutered male dogs live longer than intact males.

It is for all these valid reasons that male guide dogs for the blind are routinely neutered.

The ancestry of these cross-bred dogs is known and the characteristics of the parents can be traced in the offspring. Above left: Cairn terrier × Havanais; above right: fox terrier × Manchester terrier; below left: Pointer Labrador retriever; below right: Tibetan spaniel × cocker spaniel.

In Sickness and in Health

Disadvantages of Neutering

Aside from permanent sterilization, there are no disadvantages to this procedure.

Diseases and Disorders

Diabetes

Similar to the physical effects and symptoms seen in humans, diabetes mellitus ("sugar" diabetes) manifests itself in dogs by weight loss, increased appetite and thirst, increased urinary output, an odor of acetone on the breath, and decreased ability to fight infections. Later, in the untreated or ineffectively treated diabetic dog, the eyesight, kidneys, and vascular system may become affected severely, leading to blindness, cardiac insufficiency, circulatory disturbances, and chronic kidney disease.

Managing a diabetic dog successfully takes a team effort. Your veterinarian can help establish a proper diet and the correct dosage of insulin; you will be responsible for many daily details, so that your dog's dietary intake remains constant and its urine and blood glucose are monitored regularly. After a few weeks, you and your veterinarian will have established a daily treatment regimen that will maintain your dog's health. A properly treated canine diabetic should enjoy a satisfactory life for many years after the initial diagnosis of its disease.

Tonsillitis

Sometimes these paired lymph node-like organs in the back of a dog's throat become inflamed and

Above left: Keeshod × Chow Chow; above right: Irish terrier × golden retriever. Doberman pincher predominates in the handsome dog shown below left. The precise ancestry of the puppy shown lower right is unkown, but the mixture is obviously a complete success!

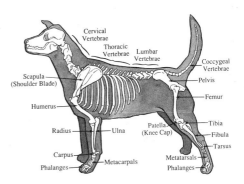

The major parts of your dog's skeleton.

greatly enlarged. Affected dogs may lose their appetites because of a sore throat, salivate excessively, and/or develop soft, dry coughs.

Inflamed tonsils often respond quickly to appropriate antibiotic therapy. If your dog has experienced recurrent or chronic tonsillitis, your veterinarian may recommend surgical removal of the tonsils, a relatively minor operation with low risk of complications. A bland, soft diet is fed for a day or two after the tonsillectomy; recovery is usually quite rapid.

Seizure Disorders

Some of the causes for seizure disorders are abnormal pressures within the skull, trauma, low blood sugar, low blood calcium, liver, and/or kidney diseases, brain tumors and abscesses, and migrating parasites. Other causes may be unclear, but some breeds of dogs are known to experience epileptiform seizures more often than other breeds. In others, trauma to the head has been implicated. Inadequate oxygen to the fetus during its passsage through the birth canal has been suggested in some cases, but this is not indesputable.

Some forms of seizure disorders are seen in young puppies but, more typically, they are observed for the first time in fully grown dogs. The

In Sickness and in Health

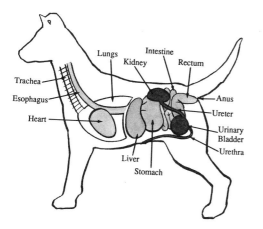

Your dog's major internal organs.

two main categories of epileptiform seizures are *grand mal* and *petit mal*. In a grand mal seizure, the affected dog usually loses consciousness, may thrash its legs, clamp its jaws tightly shut, and salivate profusely. Urine and/or feces may be released during the seizure. The duration of such an event is usually less than two minutes. In a petit mal seizure, the dog usually does not lose consciousness and may appear to be only momentarily stuporous.

A dog who displays a seizure disorder should be examined and evaluated by a veterinarian. After a thorough examination and laboratory confirmatory tests have helped elucidate the cause for seizures, the clinician may select one or more medications to administer or other course of action to treat your dog. There are some very effective oral drugs that can be used to control this condition. Many dogs with seizure disorders can live out full and satisfactory lifespans.

Kidney Diseases

Prevention: Kidney disease may be the eventual outcome of many metabolic and infectious diseases. For instance, uncontrolled diabetes, uterine infection, some liver disorders, heart failure, and adrenal diseases and leptospirosis can be manifested as kidney insufficiency or total failure. These disorders require laboratory tests and careful veterinary evaluation for their diagnosis and treatment. Although most of them may not be necessarily preventable, it is important that your dog be kept current in its routine booster vaccinations and examined at least once yearly so that those conditions that can be treated may be diagnosed early.

The diet of your dog can affect the function of its kidneys. Dogs require food containing high quality protein, but the quantity should not be excessive. Young puppies require a somewhat higher protein level because they must make body tissues during this rapid growth phase; adult dogs need only maintain body tissues. Foods with very high protein content can abnormally burden the kidneys.

The water you offer your dog must always be clean, fresh, and available at all times. The important kidney tissues can be damamged by prolonged and chronic lack of water.

Excessive salt in the diet also can damage the kidneys and other organs.

Some plants contain toxic elements that can adversely effect kidney function. It is beyond the scope of this guide to enumerate these plant species, but if you find your dog chewing your houseplants, take action immediately; correct your dog's misbehavior, eliminate the particular plants, or place them where your dog can no longer reach them.

Some common household chemicals can damage kidney tissues. Automobile antifreeze solution containing ethylene glycol is an example of such an agent; by simply storing antifreeze safely and discarding it properly, much poisoning can be avoided. Some heavy metals that are common ingredients of insecticides also are toxic to the kidneys. Some dogs, if given the opportunity, will drink or eat such products. Here again, prevention is the best medicine.

Maintenance of Dogs with Chronic Kidney Dysfunction: There are many simple things that you can do that will greatly reduce the burden of work on your dog's kidneys. Numerous special high-quality/low-quantity protein commercial products are available from your veterinarian. Alternatively, there are several excellent recipes for homemade diets for canine kidney problems. Most of these recipes are based on rice, cottage cheese, boiled chicken or lamb, and tofu (soybean cake), to which you add vitamins and low-sodium or sodium-free condiments for increasing the palatability. Your family veterinarian can help you with the choice of diet to match your dog's requirements.

A ready source of fresh water is absolutely essential because a dog with kidney disease often cannot concentrate its urine normally. Your kidney-deficient dog must *never* be deprived of water.

Due to its lack of urine concentration and the consequently greater urine volume produced daily, your dog may find it difficult to maintain its previous faultless housebroken behavior. A freeswinging "doggy door" will provide a ready exit to a backyard or run to facilitate your dog's elimination outdoors.

Dogs with even moderate kidney dysfunction, properly managed, often can live several years after their disease is diagnosed.

Urinary Bladder Disorders

Cystitis: Like humans, dogs occasionally develop inflammation of the urinary bladder. The major clinical signs of this disorder, cystitis, are frequent urination and blood in the urine. Your veterinarian, in addition to urinalysis, may employ special X-ray techniques in making the diagnosis, and probably will prescribe specific antibiotics for its treatment.

A small increase in dietary salt, as sodium chloride, may help, but be certain that you obtain your veterinarian's advice on this. Often, an increased water intake will aid in the therapy by diluting the total volume of urine. If the dog will drink it, cranberry juice may help because it increases the urine's acidity.

Kidney, Urinary Bladder, and Urethral Stones: Some dog breeds develop their own characteristic types of kidney, urinary bladder, and urethral stones. Fortunately, because of their hybrid vigor, crossbred dogs are not particularly prone to stone formation.

If they obstruct the outflow of urine, urinary stones or "calculi" can lead to severe retention, pain, and eventual death. Kidney stones usually are shaped like broad stags' antlers and form in the pelvis portion of the organ, where the urine collects before it descends the ureter into the urinary bladder. More commonly, bladder stones remain in the body of the bladder; where they induce an inflammation that often leads to bleeding. The first sign or symptom that you may note is the presence of blood-tinged urine. Often the affected dog urinates more frequently than normal. Abdominal X-ray films, called radiographs, will confirm your veterinarian's tentative diagnosis. Most urinary bladder stones require surgical removal.

The narrow tube that conducts urine from the bladder to the outside of the body is called the urethra. Stones that become lodged in the urethra require immediate veterinary medical and surgical intervention. These stones usually are small and enter the urethra from the urinary bladder, where they were formed earlier. The stones usually progress down the urethra until they reach a location where the narrow diameter will not permit further passage. Many are smaller than grains of rice, but can prove fatal if not removed promptly.

There are some nonsurgical medical measures that your veterinarian may employ to try to dislodge urethral stones, but you should be prepared for the possibility that surgery may be necessary to remove them.

In Sickness and in Health

Once the stones are removed, your veterinarian will send them to a laboratory for chemical analysis. When the analysis is known, your veterinarian may advise you to alter your dog's diet to reduce the possibility of further stone formation and a recurrence of urethral obstruction.

Disorders of the Male

Cryptorchidism: During normal embryonic and fetal development, the testicles in male puppies grow within the abdominal cavity and only descend into the scrotal sac just before birth or shortly afterward. In a relatively small number of male pups, one or both testes fail to make this descent into the scrotum. One or both may begin their short journey, only to stop while still in the body cavity; others may complete their travel through the inguinal canals, but stop short and become lodged just beneath the skin of the lower flank, or groin region. This condition is called cryptorchidism (Crypt = hidden; orchid = referring to the testicles). In order for the testicles of most mammals to produce high quality sperm successfuly, they must be kept at a temperature of slightly less than that of the deep body core. Most bilateral cryptorchid testicles are sterile organs, but if only one testicle is retained, the other may produce fertile sperm. Interestingly, there is a direct relationship between cryptorchidism and testicular tumor formation; those testicles retained within the body or beneath the skin of the groin have a much higher incidence of tumor formation. Although the affected testicles may not produce viable sperm, they can, however, produce male hormones in a relatively normal fashion and affected dogs possess male secondary characteristics and behavior.

Careful breeding studies have shown that this condition is genetically linked and thus, inherited. It is for this reason that a unilateral or bilateral cryptorchid should never be used for a stud dog. His sons would have a greater chance of being cryptorchid, and both sons and daughters would be carrying his

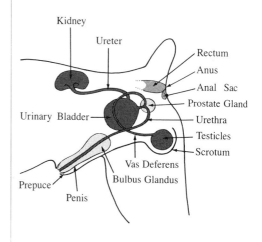

The genitourinary system of a male dog.

genes for this defect and, consequently, would pass them on to *their* offspring.

Retained testicles should be surgically removed once the affected dog has matured. This surgery should be performed at about one year of age. The opposite testicle can be removed at the same time or, alternatively, the dog can be vasectomized to prevent him from distributing his defective genes to future generations.

Testicular Tumors: Many testicular tumors are first discovered by your family veterinarian during your dog's annual physical examination and booster vaccinations.

Most of these growths are seen in dogs of at least middle age; the tumors occur with greatest frequency in dogs of eleven to fourteen years old. This disorder is rare in younger males, although there is one type that specifically affects very young dogs.

The treatment of choice generally is to surgically remove the testicle in which the tumor is growing. Ideally, the tissue is submitted for microscopic examination by a veterinary pathologist to ascertain whether the tumor was malignant or benign.

Early castration will eliminate the possibility of testicular tumors. By the age at which most of these masses affect dogs, the loss of one—or both—testicles should not result in significant behavioral changes in your pet.

Prostate Disorders: Because it possesses a prostate gland much like that of human males and lives long enough for tumors to develop, the dog is one of the few domestic animals in which prostate disease is common.

The prostate gland is dependent upon male hormones secreted by the testicles, therefore, prostate disorders, particularly cancer, are almost always confined to intact, nonneutered dogs. As the intact dog ages, there is a marked tendency for the prostate gland, which is located just behind the neck of the urinary bladder, to become enlarged. Affected dogs may experience difficulty when passing their urine or feces. Usually this prostatic enlargement is unrelated to tumor growth, although tumors may arise in such an enlarged organ.

More commonly, the prostate becomes infected and may even develop abscesses that are painful to the dog, especially when it strains to have a bowel movement.

Simple benign prostatic enlargement often is treated by either castration or female hormone (estrogen) therapy. From my point of view as a veterinary surgeon, castration is the preferred treatment because it is accompanied by the fewest and mildest secondary effects. Similarly, the medical and surgical management of prostatic infections often includes neutering.

Two disorders related to the canine prostate are perineal hernia and perianal gland tumors. Castration is a part of the treatment by which each of these conditions is corrected.

Most veterinary surgeons recommend neutering male dogs early in life. Because this simple procedure assures the owner that the pet, though sterile, will live a far healthier life than his intact kin it should be given serious consideration.

Disorders of the Scrotum: The canine scrotum, which is covered with sensitive skin, occasionally becomes inflamed when the dog sits on or in an irritating substance, becomes sunburned, or infected. Under most circumstances, the inflamed skin can be treated with soothing antiinflammatory topical ointments, creams, or lotions prescribed by a veterinarian.

Scrotal tumors are seen in older dogs, but they are not particularly common. Some of these tumors are thought to result from exposure to environmental carcinogens, such as certain chemicals. Surgery usually is effective if the disease is identified early.

Disorders of the Penis and Prepuce: Because dogs are not circumcised, their penises remain moist at all times. Often this moist and warm environment becomes inflamed and infected with common bacteria, resulting in a chronic discharge. This relatively minor but annoying condition is called *balanoposthitis.* The more your dog licks his infected organ, the more organisms will gain entrance to this optimal site in which bacteria, yeasts, and fungi flourish.

Sometimes a discharge signals the presence of one or more foreign bodies that have gained entrance to the penile sheath, called the prepuce. These foreign bodies can be bristly hairs, barbed weedy plant seeds called "foxtails," particles of coarse sand, and so forth.

If you notice a discharge from your dog's prepuce, your veterinarian should be consulted. Various solutions to this unpleasant condition exist, and you can adopt one that is most appropriate for you and your male dog.

Sometimes a dog will injure its prepuce and/or penis when he jumps over a fence. The prepuce is easily lacerated in this way. If you notice that the skin or the penis itself is traumatized, consult your veterinarian.

In Sickness and in Health

Disorders of the Female

Intact bitches may develop the identical diseases that women develop: ovarian infections, cysts, and tumors; oviductal infections, cysts and tumors; uterine infections and tumors; vaginal infections and tumors; and other miscellaneous conditions. Of course, most of these maladies can be prevented by having your bitch spayed early in life.

Ovarian Disorders: Ovarian tumors are not rare in bitches and usually make their presence known by inducing abnormal behavior and/or physical signs of irregular estrous cycling. Some tumors can reach enormous size.

Some of these masses can be seen or felt as firm, usually round protrusions within your bitch's abdomen and are discovered when you stroke or examine your pet. Ovarian tumors occasionally reach enormous size: I once operated upon a German shepherd bitch whose left ovary weighed over 14 pounds! Your family veterinarian should be consulted if you find any such lump or mass.

When ovarian and oviductal infections, which are less common, are present, abdominal pain, fever and sterility result.

Uterine Disorders: Uterine infection, called *pyometritis* or *pyometra*, is the most common disorder of the canine female reproductive tract. Often the uterine "horns" and body fill with pus, which, because the cervix is closed, cannot drain through the vaginal canal. At other times, the cervix opens and the exudate formed within the uterus drains as a thick, foul-smelling discharge from the vagina. In either case, affected bitches may exhibit fever, lethargy, lack of appetite, abdominal distension, and greatly increased thirst. There is always the potential danger that the diseased uterus will rupture into the abdomen and cause severe peritonitis. If you suspect that your bitch has a uterine infection, you should have her examined immediately.

Once a bitch has suffered a severe uterine infection, her potential fertility often is substantially reduced and although there are some nonsurgical methods for treating uterine infections, a total

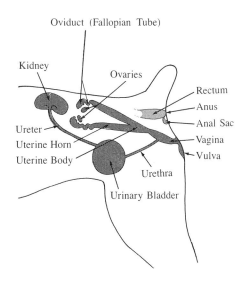

The genitourinary system of a female dog.

removal of the ovaries and uterus usually proves to be necessary.

Uterine tumors are less common, but they are, nonetheless, encountered in veterinary surgical practice. Most of these tumors are benign, but a few are found to be malignant.

Vaginal Disorders: Tumors, cysts, infections, mucosal lining protrusions, and foreign bodies are some of the more common ailments affecting the canine vagina. Many signal their presence by discharges. Protrusions of the lining of the vagina during the height of the estrus phase of the estrous cycle may be exhibited by some bitches. Although alarming to the observer, these protrusions will regress spontaneously after ovulation. Once this condition occurs during one estrus, it is common for it to recur during subsequent cycles.

Wild grasses abound in some areas of the United States, and their awned seeds can gain entrance to the vagina. These elongated seeds have barbed outer seed coats that cause them to travel in a forward direction only; because these seeds have such sharply pointed ends, they can actually penetrate the tough walls of the vagina and enter the abdominal cavity or migrate to other anatomic sites where they cause severe infections. Often surgery is required to remove the foreign body.

Disorders of the Ear

Infections: Crossbred dogs with naturally short uncropped ear flaps tend to carry their ears high enough to permit adequate air circulation into and out of the deeper ear canal structures. Ear infections caused by bacteria, yeasts, and other fungi are encountered most often, therefore, in dogs with long and pendant ear flaps.

Ear infections most often manifest themselves by head shaking, foul-smelling discharges, pain that is indicated by your dog's pawing at its ear, and vocalizing with cries or moans. These same signs may suggest that a foreign body has entered the ear canal.

If you suspect an ear infection, have your dog examined by a veterinarian. Be prepared to allow your pet to be anesthetized while its ears are thoroughly examined, cleansed, and medicated. Often the ears may be so painful that the affected dog will not permit a veterinarian to examine and treat the problem properly unless anesthesia is employed.

Foreign Bodies: As your dog runs or walks through tall wild grass or weeds whose seeds are protected by tough barbed outer coats called awns, it can pick up foreign bodies that easily enter the ear canal. To examine the interior of the ear canal, the veterinarian will insert an otoscope, an illuminated instrument fitted with a conelike speculum. Quite often because of the acute pain that some foreign bodies can produce, your dog will not permit this examination procedure, and it will have to be briefly anesthetized. If a foreign body is found during this inspection, a special long forceps is used to grasp and withdraw the offending object from the canal. After the ear canals are free of foreign matter, they are cleaned and medicated with antiinflammatory and antibiotic ointment.

Aural Hematomas: Sometimes a dog will shake its ears so vigorously that it will sustain an injury to one or more of the blood vessels between the layers of tissue that cover the cartilaginous tissue of the flap. When this happens, the blood escapes from the damaged vessel and creates a large blood "blister," called a hematoma. Usually these hematomas are relatively painless after the initial injury, but are cosmetically unacceptable. If not drained, the hematoma will eventually shrink and cause the affected ear flap to become deformed, creating a "cauliflower" ear.

Surgical correction is the treatment of choice for most of these ear flap hematomas. Your veterinarian may advise you to wait 48 to 72 hours after the initial injury. This will allow the bleeding into the hematoma to cease and the firm clot to form.

At the time of surgery, your veterinarian also will examine your dog's ear canals to determine the cause for the head shaking that initiated the hematoma and then treat it.

If the surgery is performed correctly, the postsurgical cosmetic appearance of an ear-flap hematoma is quite acceptable.

Some nonsurgical treatments for aural hematomas have been proposed and, at the time of this writing, are being evaluated for their long-term effects as compared with prompt surgical care.

Ear Mites and Ticks: Pawing at the ear, head shaking, and the presence of a dark, semi-dry, often profuse discharge within the ear canal are signs of ear mite or tick infestation.

Your dog is unlikely to suffer from these highly selective parasites that are distant cousins to spiders unless it lives with a cat whose ears are infested with ear mites, or has access to wilderness areas where ear ticks abound.

Treatment for ear mite infestation is thorough cleansing of the ear canals, followed by the instillation of an ointment or aqueous solution that will eradicate any mites or their eggs.

Ear ticks are removed physically with forceps inserted through an illuminated ear speculum and otoscope. Once the adult ticks are removed, ear mite medication is placed into the ear canals to destroy any eggs or larval ticks.

Deafness: It is entirely normal for an aging dog to lose some of its hearing as the years pass. If your young dog appears to be growing deaf, you should have it examined by a veterinarian. The cause may be as simple as an accumulation of ear wax obstructing the ear canals adjacent to the ear drum. Tumors and foreign bodies are other causes for temporary deafness.

Disorders of the Eyes

Injuries: Traumatic injuries to your dog's eyes usually result from objects in the environment such as sticks, weed seeds, and cat claw scratches. The dog's own paws and claws also can injure the delicate eye and lid tissues as the animal rubs its face. Less commonly, a dog's eyes accidently may be exposed to caustic or irritating household or garden chemicals.

Pain and excessive secretion of tears are the major signs of eye injury. The dog usually will keep its eyelid closed tightly in an attempt to protect the injured or inflamed eye.

If you know for certain that some object or chemical irritant entered your pet's eyes, immediately flush the eyes with warm water or, if you have it in your medicine cabinet, a sterile ophthalmic irrigating solution. A good substitute for this product is hard contact lens wetting solution or soft contact lens solution that does not contain trimerasol. Gently open the dog's eyelids by spreading them between the fingers of one hand and then instill or direct a fine stream of irrigating solution onto the cornea. As soon as possible, take your dog to a veterinarian for examination and evaluation of the extent of injury.

Foreign Bodies: Many weed seeds have sharply barbed awns and seed coats that can severely lacerate an otherwise undamaged cornea. Your family veterinarian can extract these objects skillfully without creating further trauma, and then the tissues can be examined with special staining techniques to reveal the extent of any damage. Therefore, if you can see a foreign object protruding from between your dog's eyelids do not attempt to remove it yourself.

Infectious Canine Hepatitis-related Corneal Changes: A sudden loss of clarity in one or both corneas is a frequent sequel to infection with the virus of infectious canine hepatitis. The corneas become milky-blue. Even without therapy, this cloudiness usually will clear within a few days. Your veterinarian can prescribe medication that will hasten this clearing.

Cataracts: When the crystalline lens becomes opaque, it is called a cataract. Normally, the substance of the crystalline lens is absolutely clear, and light passes through the lens, to be focused on the retina at the back of the eye. Two major types of cataracts are known: juvenile and mature. The juvenile form usually occurs rather suddenly and prior to the eighth year of life. The mature form develops much more slowly and is usually seen in dogs at least nine or ten years old. Cataracts can form with alarming rapidity in some cases of severe diabetes. These lens opacities may be the first outward sign of diabetes noticed by an owner.

It is unusual for crossbred dogs to develop juvenile cataracts but, if they are seen, you should have your dog examined by a veterinarian skilled in the treatment of eye diseases.

Unless there are secondary changes within the eyes, such as glaucoma, little need be done to treat mature cataracts. They are only a consequence of aging gracefully.

Glaucoma: Glaucoma is defined as an abnormal increase of pressure within the eye. In order to maintain the internal structures in their anatomically proper locations within the globelike eye, each normal eye must have a fluid pressure slightly higher than that of the atmosphere. This fluid is constantly secreted by specialized tissues within the eyes. If anything acts to block the normal drainage of fluid from the eye, the pressure within that eye will gradually or suddenly increase. Then the eye will enlarge to accommodate the increased fluid volume and pressure. As this happens, delicate nervous tissues, particularly those of the retina, can suffer irreparable damage, and total blindness can ensue.

Glaucoma can be either acute, in that its onset is sudden, or gradual and chronic. The result is the same, but whereas the chronic form is painless, the acute form can be very painful.

Each annual physical examination your dog receives at the time of its routine booster immunizations should always include an ophthalmologic examination.

Disorders of the Coat and Skin

Flea-bite Allergy: One of the most frequent disorders of the skin of dogs is allergy to flea saliva that is injected into the skin at the time that the fleas take their blood meals. Many dogs respond to this potent protein allergen by making specific antibodies to it. Within a variable period of time, each new flea bite prompts an intense reaction of local irritation and itching. Sometimes an affected dog will mutilate its own skin by trying to relieve the discomfort; in these instances, a short course of antiinflammatory cortisone injections or tablets may be indicated to afford your dog temporary relief and allow its skin to heal.

Routine use of a high quality flea and tick spray or powder is the simplest method for avoiding flea-bite allergy dermatitis. In severe cases of this skin disorder, a single flea bite can arouse an intense allergic reaction. In such a case, your veterinarian may wish to employ a course of desensitizing injections with one of several flea extracts.

Contact Dermatitis and Atopy: Wool carpeting, certain plant fibers, pollens, soaps, and chemical cleansers are substances in the home and outdoor environment to which some dogs acquire an allergic sensitivity.

The symptoms of contact dermatitis in the dog are the same as those seen in humans exposed to poison ivy, oak, and sumac. After the skin has been sensitized by previous exposure, subsequent contact with the allergen in question will result in an often intense reaction that is marked by redness, swelling, and itchiness.

In treating this form of allergy, gently wash the skin to remove any residual allergen, then apply soothing lotions containing cortisone or cortisonelike medication. In severe cases, your veterinarian can inject cortisone for quicker relief of the allergic reaction.

Atopy usually is elicited by the inhalation of allergens in the form of dusts, plant pollens, or animal danders. Atopy resembles many of the signs seen in humans allergic to these same substances.

Food Allergy-related Dermatitis: Milk products, eggs, poultry, meat products, pork, fish, and other seafood are most often implicated in dog allergies. The effects of allergy to certain foods may be almost immediately apparent: breathing difficulties, skin rashes ("hives"), excessive secretion of tears and saliva. In a few dogs, the reaction may prove fatal, but these cases usually have had a previous history of acute illness after eating certain foods. Most cases of food allergy dermatitis end spontaneously; others may need the use of antihistamines, cortisonelike drugs, or adrenaline to abolish the signs and symptoms of the acute reaction.

Hypothyroidism: A deficiency of thyroid function can result in the development of scaly skin with rough hair coat. The fur may appear overly dry or excessively greasy, depending upon the state of thyroid function. During the evaluation of your dog's physical condition, a battery of thyroid gland function tests will be requested by your veterinarian. After these test results are studied, a regimen of treatment will be selected. Once the cause for your dog's thyroid function is determined and treated, the prognosis for recovery is favorable.

Skin Tumors: The majority of skin tumors in dogs are benign; others are highly malignant and behave aggressively. They may be solitary or multiple, slowly growing or rapidly spreading, pigmented or pigment-free. Some breeds are more prone to developing these lesions than others. Often found when dogs are groomed and the fur is clipped, the previously hidden lesions may be scraped and bleed.

Take your dog to its veterinarian for an evaluation and/or surgical removal of skin tumors. The ideal time for surgery is when the skin tumors are still small because they can be removed most easily and leave only small scars. However, even large, broad-based tumors can be removed. Your veterinarian will probably submit each suspected tumor to a pathologist for a diagnosis of its type and potential for future aggressive behavior.

Sometimes tumors arise in the fatty tissues just beneath the skin. These masses may be solitary or multiple, and usually can be moved freely as the skin is slipped back and forth over them. Most of these tumors are of fatty origin and are called lipomas. This type of tumor occurs more frequently in dogs who are at least middle-aged. The majority are benign and can be removed easily by a veterinary surgeon.

Disorders of the Anal Sacs

Preventing Problems: Each time the dog defecates, there is a little secretion from these twin saclike structures that lie beneath the skin covering the anal sphincter. These secretions of the paired anal sacs are employed to scent mark a dog's territory and, to a lesser extent, to help lubricate the anal canal during passage of stools. If a dog is obese, the sacs move into the soft fatty tissue and return after the stools are passed; if the anal sac secretions are thus not released, they often become dried. After a variable period of time, this dried material becomes impacted, and the sac becomes inflamed. Dogs with impacted or irritated anal sacs will "scoot" on their rumps to help relieve their discomfort.

One of the easiest means for preventing anal sac problems is to keep your dog from becoming obese.
Impaction and Abscesses: Because of their close-

ness to the anus, the anal sacs may become infected with a variety of bacterial organisms and form painful abscesses (inflamed tissue with accumulated pus). An abscessed anal sac may form a draining opening to the outside. If your dog is experiencing anal sac discomfort, consult your veterinarian for evaluation and treatment.

Treatment of Impacted or Abscessed Anal Sacs: Often these sacs can be drained and treated with antiinflammatory ointments and antibiotic injections. A gloved finger is inserted into the anus and each sac is drained separately. This procedure is most effectively performed by a veterinarian.

In chronic or severe cases of anal saculitis, your veterinarian may advise the surgical removal of both of these nonessential organs. Once the anal sacs are removed, you will find that your dog will have lost much of its previous "doggy" odor. Some people elect to prevent problems by having their dogs' anal sacs removed when a spay or neutering operation is performed, thus requiring that the animal be anesthetized only once. This is precisely what I did with the last three dogs with whom we have shared our home.

Disorders of the Perianal or Circumanal Glands: Separate and distinct from the paired anal sacs are small perianal or circumanal glands that lie just beneath the skin of the anus. These structures occasionally become infected or involved in tumor formation.

Infections: Abscesses and fistulas (abnormal passages from an abscess or organ) may develop in these glands. They are troublesome to treat effectively because this region of the body is not conducive to strict hygiene.

Home treatment employing the application of hot compresses and antibiotic and antiinflammatory ointments may be all that is necessary but, more often, aggressive surgical intervention is required. Your family veterinarian should be consulted for a professional evaluation.

Tumors: Perianal gland tumors are much more common than are abscesses and fistulas. Male hormone, which is secreted by the testicles, tends to foster the growth of these tumors and, therefore they are encountered more often in the male than in the bitch.

Some perianal gland tumors are benign and others are aggressively malignant. Because some otherwise benign tumors are characterized by small clusters of malignant cells, these tumors should be removed early and examined by a veterinary pathologist.

Surgery may not be enough in some very aggressive perianal gland tumors, and radiation therapy is indicated. Fortunately, this tumor type is usually responsive to radiation, and the post-treatment course of recovery is usually satisfactory.

If your intact male dog develops a perianal gland tumor, your veterinarian may advise that you authorize castration of your pet at the time of its anal surgery. In most cases, this is entirely warranted.

Arthritis

Arthritis may develop in one or more of its joints as your dog ages. The most common age-related arthritis is called *osteoarthritis*, and it usually develops gradually over a period of months or years. Younger dogs may acquire arthritic joints from bacterial infections or traumatic accidents, and these require the immediate care of a veterinarian. **Prevention:** Because each ounce of extra weight is an additional burden on its many joints, the most effective way to prevent, or at least forestall, osteoarthritis is to offer your dog adequate exercise. Swimming is an excellent means for exercising your pet's entire body. Making sure that your dog has a warm and draft-free place to sleep also may retard the development and pain of arthritis. **Medical Management:** Adrenal cortical steroid hormones and aspirin used to be the mainstays of veterinary medical management of canine arthritis. More recently, a group of "nonsteroidal antiinflammatory" drugs have shown great promise in reducing joint inflammation and pain in dogs. Once a

diagnosis of your dog's lameness is made, your veterinarian can prescribe one or more medications.

Are Dog Diseases Dangerous to Humans?

Except for rabies, bacterial infections arising out of dog-bite wounds, and exposure to infected urine from active cases of canine leptospirosis that can be hazardous to humans, there are few diseases that dogs and their owners share. The more common viral diseases of dogs, such as canine distemper, infectious canine hepatitis, parainfluenza, parvoviral gastroenteritis, and coronaviral gastroenteritis are not transmissible to humans. Several worm and protozoan parasites also affect people, but routine hygiene greatly lessens exposure to these organisms. Some fungal skin diseases such as ringworm, and the mite infestation known as scabies or mange can be transmitted from dogs to people—and *vice versa*.

There are probably on record as many cases of dogs contracting diseases from their owners as the reverse. A number of cases of canine tuberculosis have been traced to their infected owners, but these are not common today because tuberculosis no longer is a widely endemic disease in the United States.

Exercise for You and Your Dog

The amount and type of routine exercise can be tailored to the tolerance of both of you for physical exercise. At the least, a brisk walk around the block will be mutually beneficial. A run in the park or a swim in a nearby lake in good weather will maintain your dog's muscle tone and psychological balance. The amount of exertion should be adjusted to its abilities as your dog ages.

Gradually increasing exposure to the pavement over a period of several weeks can allow your pet's foot and toe pads to become accustomed to the extra wear. In very warm or humid weather, allow your dog to rest at intervals so that it can dissipate its increased body temperature. Dogs do not have sweat glands distributed over their entire bodies and must rely upon panting to exhaust the bulk of excess heat. Remember to provide your dog free access to fresh water.

A Veterinarian's View of Euthanasia: A Last Act of Love

> **Euthanasia**, from the Greek words meaning *good + death*; the act of painlessly inducing death, for reasons of mercy, of patients suffering from incurable and distressing disease or injury.

As a veterinary surgeon, I have always appreciated the enormous privilege of being able to end the suffering of some of my patients. We live at a time when it is possible to extend the life of many patients, but we always must be acutely aware that by doing so we also may be extending their exposure to intense and constant pain. In other words, too often attempts to prolong the life of a patient result only in prolonged dying. No humane person would knowingly subject another creature to suffering, but often during my professional career I have not been able to persuade an otherwise loving pet owner to finally "let go" and allow an animal companion to die and thus be released from a terribly painful existence. In many cases it was clear to me that the reason for this reluctance to part from an obviously suffering pet was based solely upon the owner's sense of impending loss, and little or no consideration was given to the plight of the animal.

To permit euthanasia is a deeply personal decision and can be made only after great emotional soul-searching. The caring veterinarian realizes that euthanasia is a terribly painful choice, and stands ready to be supportive when that decision must be made. Our profession can, if called upon, end our patients' suffering by acts of *commission*; our physician colleague must rely solely upon acts of *omission*. That difference is of immense importance and we do not consider it lightly.

Dealing with the Loss of a Much-loved Pet

The most difficult thing I must face, as a veterinarian engaged in clinical practice, is having to tell an owner that a pet either has died or will soon die. This situation has always been most heartfelt when the owner lived alone with the pet as an only companion.

To grieve over the loss of a loved one is absolutely normal, whether that loved one was a fellow human being or a pet animal.

There is increasing interest and research today into the "human-animal bond" that exists between people and their pets. For some persons, a loved pet is an "anchor to reality" that for one or more reasons serves as a surrogate for human companionship.

If you are experiencing difficulty in deciding whether to allow your loved pet to die peacefully, refer to the list of professionals trained to help you in this time of personal loss. Their names are printed in the section of Useful Addresses. Titles of several publications are also included for your reference.

Useful Books and Addresses

Counselors Dealing with the Human-Animal Bond

The following professionals are specially trained to deal with people facing the imminent or recent loss of a loved pet. Their services are free or very modest in cost. Each of these sources can also furnish you with information regarding support groups to help you over a difficult period.

Suzanne Arguello
School of Veterinary Medicine
Colorado State University
Fort Collins, Colorado 80521
(303) 493-0415

Dr. Leo K. Bustad
College of Veterinary Medicine
Washington State University
Pullman, Washington 99163
(509) 335-1297

Susan Cohen
The Animal Medical Center
510 East 62nd Street
New York, New York 10021
(212) 838-8100

Dr. Lynette Hart; Bonnie S. Mader, MSW
School of Veterinary Medicine
University of California
Davis, California 95616
(916) 752-7418

Dr. Ralph Holcomb
School of Veterinary Medicine
University of Minnesota
Minneapolis, Minnesota 55455
(612) 624-4747

Dr. Victoria Voith
School of Veterinary Medicine
University of Pennsylvania
Philadelphia, Pennsylvania 19104
(215) 898-4525

Useful Literature

Dealing with the Loss of a Pet

Nieburg, Herbert, A. and Arlene Fischer *Pet Loss: A Thoughtful Guide for Adults and Children.* Harper and Row, New York, 1982.

Quackenbush, James, E. and D. Graveline *When Your Pet Dies: How to Cope with Your Feelings.* Simon and Schuster, New York, 1985

Rosenberg, Marc, A. *Companion Animal Loss and Pet Owner Grief.* ALPO Center, 1985. Library of Congress Catalog Card Number 85-73830

White, Betty. *Pet Love.* Morrow, New York, 1983.

Pet Loss and Human Emotion. American Veterinary Medical Assocation, 930 North Meacham Road, Schaumberg, Illinois 60196. (Free)

Dogs and Dog Care

Alderton, David *The Dog Care Manual.* Barron's Educational Series, Hauppauge, New York, 1986.

Baer, Ted *Communicating with Your Dog.* Barron's Educational Series, Hauppauge, New York, 1984.

Frye, Fredric L. *First Aid for Your Dog.* Barron's Educational Series, Hauppauge, New York, 1987.

Lorenz, Konrad Z. *Man Meets Dog.* Penguin Books, London and New York, 1967.

Ullman, Hans-J. *The New Dog Handbook.* Barron's Educational Series, Hauppauge, New York, 1984.

Touring with Towser: a directory of hotels and motels that accommodate guests with dogs. Gaines TWT, P.O. Box 8172, Kankakee, Illinois 60901 (price: $1.50)

Index

Index

Perfect for Pet Owners!

"Clear, concise...written in simple, nontechnical language."

—*Booklist*

AFRICAN GRAY PARROTS Wolter (3773-1)
AMAZON PARROTS Lantermann (4035-X)
BANTAMS Fritzsche (3687-5)
BEAGLES Vriends-Parent (3829-0)
BEEKEEPING Melzer (4089-9)
BOSTON TERRIERS Bulanda (1696-3)
BOXERS Kraupa-Tuskany (4036-8)
CANARIES Frisch (2614-4)
CATS Fritzsche (2421-4)
CHINCHILLAS Röder-Thiede (1471-5)
CHOW-CHOWS Atkinson (3952-1)
COCKATIELS Wolter (2889-9)
COCKATOOS Lantermann & Lantermann (4159-3)
COCKER SPANIELS Sucher (1478-2)
COLLIES Sundstrom & Sundstrom (1875-3)
CONURES Vriends (4880-6)
DACHSHUNDS Fiedelmeier (1843-5)
DALMATIANS Ditto (4605-6)
DISCUS FISH Giovanette (4669-2)
DOBERMAN PINSCHERS Gudas (2999-2)
DOGS Wegler (4822-9)
DOVES Vriends (1855-9)
DWARF RABBITS Wegler (1352-2)
ENGLISH SPRINGER SPANIELS Ditto (1778-1)
FEEDING AND SHELTERING BACKYARD BIRDS
  Vriends (4252-2)
FEEDING AND SHELTERING EUROPEAN BIRDS
  von Frisch (2858-9)
FERRETS Morton (2976-3)
GERBILS Gudas (3725-1)
GERMAN SHEPHERDS Antesberger (2982-8)
GOLDEN RETRIEVERS Sucher (3793-6)
GOLDFISH Ostrow (2975-5)
GREAT DANES Stahlkuppe (1418-9)
GUINEA PIGS Bielfeld (2629-2)
GUPPIES, MOLLIES, PLATYS
  Hieronimus (1497-9)
HAMSTERS Fritzsche (2422-2)
IRISH SETTERS Stahlkuppe (4663-3)
KEESHONDEN Stahlkuppe (1560-6)
LABRADOR RETRIEVERS Kern (3792-8)

LHASA APSOS Wehrman (3950-5)
LIZARDS IN THE TERRARIUM Jes (3925-4)
LONGHAIRED CATS Müller (2803-1)
LONG-TAILED PARAKEETS Wolter (1351-4)
LORIES AND LORIKEETS Vriends (1567-3)
LOVEBIRDS Vriends (3726-X)
MACAWS Sweeney (4768-0)
MICE Bielfeld (2921-6)
MINIATURE PIGS Storer (1356-5)
MUTTS Frye (4126-7)
MYNAHS von Frisch (3688-3)
NONVENOMOUS SNAKES Trutnau (5632-9)
PARAKEETS Wolter (2423-0)
PARROTS Wolter (4823-7)
PERSIAN CATS Müller (4405-3)
PIGEONS Vriends (4044-9)
POMERANIANS Stahlkuppe (4670-6)
PONIES Kraupa-Tuskany (2856-2)
POODLES Ullmann & Ullmann (2812-0)
PUGS Maggitti (1824-9)
RABBITS Fritzsche (2615-2)
RATS Himsel (4535-1)
SCHNAUZERS Frye (3949-1)
SCOTTISH FOLD CATS Maggitti (4999-3)
SHAR-PEI Ditto (4834-2)
SHEEP Müller (4091-0)
SHETLAND SHEEPDOGS Sucher (4264-6)
SIAMESE CATS Collier (4764-8)
SIBERIAN HUSKIES Kenn (4265-4)
SMALL DOGS Kriechbaumer (1951-2)
SNAKES Griehl (2813-9)
SPANIELS Ullmann & Ullmann (2424-9)
TROPICAL FISH Stadelmann (4700-1)
TURTLES Wilke (4702-8)
WATER PLANTS IN THE AQUARIUM Scheurmann
  (3926-2)
WEST HIGHLAND WHITE TERRIERS
  Bolle-Kleinbub (1950-4)
YORKSHIRE TERRIERS Kriechbaumer & Grünn
  (4406-1)
ZEBRA FINCHES Martin (3497-X)

Paperback, 6 ½ x 7 ⅞ with over 50 illustrations (20-plus color photos)   Barron's ISBN prefix: 0-8120

Barron's Educational Series, Inc. • 250 Wireless Blvd., Hauppauge, NY 11788
Call toll-free: 1-800-645-3476 • In Canada: Georgetown Book Warehouse
34 Armstrong Ave., Georgetown, Ont. L7G 4R9 • Call toll-free: 1-800-247-7160

Order these titles from your favorite book or pet store.